ROBERT HENRYSON

The Testament of Cresseid & Seven Fables

translated by Seamus Heaney

faber and faber

First published in 2009
by Faber and Faber Ltd
Bloomsbury House
74–77 Great Russell Street
London WC1B 3DA

Typeset by Faber and Faber Ltd
Printed in England by T. J. International Ltd, Padstow, Cornwall

A CIP record for this book
is available from the British Library

ISBN 978–0–571–25254–1 (limited edition)
ISBN 978–0–571–24928–2

10 9 8 7 6 5 4 3 2 1

Contents

Introduction

Little enough is known about Robert Henryson, 'a schoolmaster of Dunfermline' and master poet in the Scots language: born perhaps in the 1420s, he was dead by 1505, the year his younger contemporary William Dunbar mourned his passing in 'Lament for the Makars'. In a couplet where the rhyme tolls very sweetly and solemnly, Dunbar says that death 'In Dunfermelyne . . . has done roun [whispered]/ To Maister Robert Henrisoun', although here the title 'Maister' has more to do with the deceased man's status as a university graduate than with his profession as a teacher or his reputation as the author of three major narrative poems – *The Testament of Cresseid*, *The Moral Fables* and *Orpheus and Eurydice* – as well as a number of shorter lyrics including the incomparable (and probably untranslatable) 'Robyn and Makene'.

The honorific title is an early indication that Henryson was a learned poet, even though his learning, according to one distinguished editor, would have been considered very old-fashioned by the standards of contemporary Continental humanism. 'In so far as the terms have any meaning,' Denton Fox writes in his 1987 edition of *The Poems*, 'Henryson belongs firmly to the Middle Ages, not to the Renaissance.' Yet he belongs also in the eternal present of the perfectly pitched, a poet whose knowledge of life is matched by the range of his art, whose constant awareness of the world's hardness and injustice is mitigated by his irony, tender-heartedness, and ever-ready sense of humour.

Most important of all, however, is Henryson's 'sound of sense', the way his voice is (as he might have put it) 'mingit' with the verse forms, the way it can modulate from insinuation to instruction, from high-toned earnestness to wily familiarity – and it was this sensation of intimacy with a speaker at once sober and playful that inspired me to begin putting the not very difficult Scots language of his originals into rhymed stanzas of more immediately accessible English.

But why begin at all, the reader may ask, since the Scots is not, in fact, so opaque? Anybody determined to have a go at it can turn to Denton Fox's edition or to the Henryson section of Douglas Gray's conveniently annotated *Selected Poems of Robert Henryson and William Dunbar*. Reading his work in this way may be a slow process – eyes to-ing and fro-ing between text and glossary, getting used to the unfamiliar orthography, ears testing out and taking in the measure of the metre – but it is still a fulfilling experience. And yet people who are neither students nor practising poets are unlikely to make such a deliberate effort.

I began to make the versions of Henryson included in this book because of a combination of the three motives for translation identified by the poet and translator Eliot Weinberger. First and foremost, advocacy for the work in question, for unless this poetry is brought out of the university syllabus and on to the shelves 'a great prince in prison lies'. But Weinberger's other two motives were equally operative: refreshment from a different speech and culture, and the pleasures of 'writing by proxy'.

Re-reading Henryson some forty years after I had first encountered him as an undergraduate, I experienced what John Dryden called (in his preface to *Fables, Ancient and Modern*) a 'transfusion', and the fact that Dryden used the term in relation to his modernisation of Chaucer made it all the more applicable to my own case: what I was involved in, after all, was the modernisation of work by one of a group of Scottish poets who shared Dryden's high regard for the genius of 'The noble Chaucer, of makers flower', and who brought about a significant flowering in the literary life of Scotland during the fifteenth and early sixteenth centuries.

None of them, however, showed a greater degree of admiration for their English forebear or was more influenced by his achievement than Robert Henryson. Not only did he write *The Testament of Cresseid*, in which he explicitly acknowledges his indebtedness to Chaucer's *Troilus and Criseyde,* but in *The Testament, Orpheus and Eurydice* and the fables, he employs the rhyme royal stanza, the form established by the English poet for work of high seriousness, although it must be said that Henryson made it a fit vehicle for much homelier modes and matter.

Chaucer's *Troilus* deals with that Trojan protagonist's love for Cressida (as Shakespeare names her in his dramatisation of the story) and with Cressida's subsequent betrayal of Troilus when she abandons him and goes off with the Greek hero Diomede. Henryson takes all this as read but refers to another source which carries the story further, to the point where his Cresseid (stress on second syllable) is abandoned in her turn by Diomede. After an introduction of several attractively confidential stanzas which present the poet as an ageing man in a wintry season, no longer as erotically susceptible as he would wish, we are quickly *in medias res*, in the Greek camp with the cast-off heroine who now goes about 'available' to the rank and file 'like any common pick-up'.

Subsequently she manages to return home to her father Calchas, where she begins to recuperate in isolation, but then – disastrously – she rebukes Cupid and Venus, the god and goddess of love, blaming her comedown on them:

> O false Cupid, none is to blame but you,
> You and your mother who is love's blind goddess.
> You gave me to believe and I trusted you,
> That the seed of love was sown in my face –

and so on. And then, in a manner of speaking, all heaven breaks loose. A convocation of the planets occurs and the poet starts upon a long set-piece of characterisation and description as he introduces the gods who are the geniuses of the different planets, a passage which allows him to demonstrate rather splendidly his store of classical and medieval learning.

This interlude may hold up the action, much as a masque will in a Shakespearean play, or an Olympian scene in classical epic, but it is still thoroughly of its time – a pageant, a sequence of tableaux, reminiscent of those that rolled their way through medieval York and Chester at Easter, showing how the inhabitants of the Christian heaven were also crucially involved in the affairs of mortals on earth – not least those who, like Cresseid, had incurred the divine wrath.

Immediately then, as a result of the gods' judgement, Cresseid is stricken with leprosy and doomed to spend the rest of her life as a beggar in a leper colony, a fate which allows for another great set-piece, her lament for the way of life and the beauty she has lost; yet it is also a fate which will bring her in the painful end to an encounter with her former lover Troilus, as he returns in triumph from a victory over 'the Grecian knights'. This is one of the most famous and affecting scenes in literature, a recognition scene (as Douglas Gray observes) all the more powerful for containing no recognition:

> *Than upon him scho kest up baith hir ene –*
> *And with ane blenk it come into his thocht*
> *That he sumtime hir face befoir had sene.*
> *Bot scho was in sic plye he knew hir nocht;*
> *Yit than hir luik into his mynd had brocht*
> *The sweit visage and amorous blenking*
> *Of fair Cresseid, sumtyme his awin darling.*

> Upon him then she cast up both her eyes
> And at a glance it came into his thought
> That he some time before had seen her face
> But she was in such state he knew her not;
> Yet still into his mind her look had brought
> The features and the amorous sweet glancing
> Of fair Cresseid, one time his own, his darling.

Swiftly then the tale concludes. Troilus is overcome by an involuntary fit of trembling and showers alms of gold into Cresseid's lap, then rides away, leaving her to discover his identity from the lepers. After which she utters another love lament, then takes pen and paper to compose her testament, bequeathing her 'royall ring set with this rubie reid' to Troilus, and having settled all earthly affairs, expires in grief.

> Some said he made a tomb of marble grey
> And wrote her name on it and an inscription
> In golden letters, above where she lay
> Inside her grave. These were the words set down:
> 'Lo, fair ladies, Cresseid of Troy town,
> Accounted once the flower of womanhood,
> Of late a leper, under this stone lies dead.'

It is customary to contrast Henryson's grave handling of this tale with Chaucer's rather more beguiling treatment. Both strike a wholly mature note, but the Scottish poet's is more richly freighted with an 'ample power/ To chasten and subdue'. Weight of judgement, a tenderness that isn't clammy, a dry-eyed sympathy – these are the Henryson hallmarks, attributes of a moral understanding reluctant to moralise, yet one that is naturally and unfalteringly instructive. Henryson is a narrative poet whom you read not only for the story but for the melody of understanding in the storytelling voice. If Hugh MacDiarmid had been asked half a millennium later what be meant by saying that the kind of poetry he wanted was 'the poetry of a grown man', he could have pointed straight to *The Testament*.

This was also the poetry of a man whose imaginative sympathy prevailed over the stock responses of his time. To his contemporaries, Henryson's entitlement as a poet would have depended to a considerable extent on his intellectual attainments, his education in astronomy and astrology, in matters legal and literary, but from our point of view he proves himself more by his singular compassion for the character of Cresseid. Available to him all along was the rhetoric of condemnation, the trope of woman as the daughter of Eve, temptress, snare, Jezebel. But Henryson eschews this pulpit-speak:

> And yet whatever men may think or say
> Contemptuously about your quick compliance
> I will excuse to what extent I may
> Your womanhood, wisdom and loveliness
> Which the whim of fortune put to such distress.

There is a unique steadiness about the movement of Henryson's stanzas, a fine and definite modulation between the colloquial and the graver, more considered elements of his style. If his rhetoric is elevated, his sounding line neverthless goes deep:

> *Ane doolie sessoun to ane cairfull dyte*
> *Suld correspond and be equivalent:*
> *Richt sa it was quhen I began to wryte*
> *This tragedie…*

Here the phonetic make-up contributes strongly if stealthily to the emotional power of the declaration. The 'oo' in 'doolie' makes the doleful meaning of the word even more doleful, and the gloom of it is just that little bit gloomier when the 'oo' sound gets repeated in 'sessoun'; and then comes that succession of reluctant, braking

Scottish 'r's in 'cairfull' and 'correspond' and (especially) 'tragedie'. Foreboding about the grievous story he has to tell is already present in the undermusic of what purports to be a mere throat-clearing exercise by a professional. And if my own sense-clearing could not hope to capture fully that tolling tragic note, it could at least echo the metre and approximate the rhyme:

> A gloomy time, a poem full of hurt
> Should correspond and be equivalent.
> Just so it was when I began my work
> On this retelling . . .

What had actually started me 'on this retelling' was the chance sighting of a Henryson text in a British Library exhibition called *Chapter and Verse*. This included an early illustrated manuscript of his 'moral fable', 'The Cock and the Jasp', and I was so taken by the jaunty, canty note of its opening lines that I felt an urge to get it into my own words. I was further encouraged in this because, a little while earlier, after I had given a reading of my *Beowulf* translation in the Lincoln Center in New York, the director had suggested that I should translate some other narrative that could be performed by an actor. Very soon afterwards, therefore, I began to do 'The Cock and the Jasp' into English stanzas, and even thought of preparing a Henryson selection to be called *Four Fables and a Testament*. So, working on the principle that the bigger job should be tackled first, I immediately faced into the 'tragedie'.

I enjoyed the work because Henryson's language led me back into what might be called 'the hidden Scotland' at the back of my own ear. The speech I grew up with in mid-Ulster carried more than a trace of Scottish vocabulary and as a youngster I was familiar with Ulster Scots idioms and pronunciations across the River Bann in County Antrim. I was therefore entirely at home with Henryson's 'sound of sense', so much in tune with his note and his pace and his pitch that I developed a strong inclination to hum along with him. Hence the decision to translate the poems with rhyme and metre, to match as far as possible the rhetoric and the roguery of the originals, and in general 'keep the accent'.

After I read the full collection of thirteen fables, however, I realised that to present only four of them would be to sell Henryson short. The collection contains some of his fiercest allegories of human existence – 'The Preaching of the Swallow' and 'The Toad and the Mouse' – as well as some of his gentlest presentations of decency in civic and domestic life – 'The Two Mice', 'The Lion and the Mouse'; but in all of these, as well as in 'The Fox, the Wolf and the Carter' and 'The Fox, the Wolf and the Farmer', there is also satire and social realism – even if the society involved is that of wild animals.

Much can be said about the sources of these tales and about the overall structure of the collection, but here it will suffice to note that while Aesop is credited throughout as the original author, the fables derive from and greatly expand on later compendia and textbooks, in particular one by Gualterus Anglicus (Walter the Englishman) and another one, the *Roman de Renart*, a well-known anthology of fox tales. Equally important, however, is the fact that these tales of tricky and innocent beasts and birds were part of the common oral culture of Europe, a store of folk wisdom as pervasive and unifying at vernacular level as the doctines and visions of Christianity were in the higher realms of scholastic culture.

Not that Henryson was indifferent to those higher registers of thought and discourse. The structure of his understanding was determined by the medieval world picture of human life situated on a plane between animal and angel, human beings a dual compound of soul and body, caught between heavenly aspiring intellect and down-dragging carnal appetite. If he was a schoolteacher, he was also a school man. If he was professionally aware of the classics, he was equally and perhaps even anxiously aware of the confessional.

In fact, much of the charm and strength of the fables comes from the way Henryson's hospitable imagination seems to enjoy open access to both the educated *lingua franca* and the subcultural codes of his late medieval world. Sometimes this adds a touch of sophisticated comedy, as when the mouse (in the final fable) launches into an argument based on the principles of physiognomy; sometimes it adds pathos, as when the swallow preaches the virtue of prudence to the doomed, ineducable little birds; sometimes it adds a touch of donnish humour, as when the wolf unexpectedly adduces his knowledge of contract law to claim owership of the oxen in 'The Fox, the Wolf and the Farmer'.

More importantly, this easy passage between the oral and learned culture, between the rhetoric of the clerks and the rascality of the beasts, establishes his world as a credible hierarchical place of social order and seasonal cycles, a world where custom and ceremony can never rule out criminality and deception or a judicious style occlude actual injustice. The stylistic reward for this inclusive vision is felt, moreover, in the nice modulation that occurs between the storytelling voice of the fable proper and the didactic voice of the 'Moralitas': if the latter is often much less confiding, more button-lipped and tendentious, this is no more than a dramatic rendering of the overall double perspective, of an intelligence stretched between the homely and the homiletic.

The genre demanded the application of a formal 'moralitas' yet the requirement also suited something strict and disciplined in Henryson's temperament, so there is integrity in the procedure rather than a mere tagging on of *sententiae*. But the richest moments in the fables are those when the natural world or the human predicament calls forth Henryson's rapture or his realism, whether it be in the dream vision of his meeting with Aesop at the beginning of 'The Lion and the Mouse' or the description of the changing seasons in 'The Preaching of the Swallow' or the verve and villainy of the fox in dialogue with the wolf prior to their duping of the carter:

> 'Still,' said the wolf, 'by banks and braes you wend
> And slink along and steal up on your prey.'
> 'Sir,' said the fox, 'you know how these things end.
> They catch my scent down wind from far away
> And scatter fast and leave me in dismay.
> They could be lying sleeping in a field
> But once I'm close they're off. It puts me wild.'

Beasts they may be, but through their agency Henryson creates a work which answers MacDiarmid's big challenging definition of poetry as 'human existence come to life'.

Acknowledgements and Notes

The translation of *The Testament of Cresseid* originally appeared in a limited edition with artwork by Hughie O'Donoghue (Enitharmon Press, 2004). Portions of the introduction to that volume have been included in the one included in this edition.

I am grateful for the commentaries, annotations and glossaries provided in *Robert Henryson: The Poems*, edited by Denton Fox (OUP, 1987) and *Selected Poems of Robert Henryson and William Dunbar*, edited by Douglas Gray (Penguin, 1998). Thanks are also due to Douglas Gray and to Penguin Books for permission to reproduce the original text of Robert Henryson's poems, as regularised and punctuated by Douglas Gray in the above-mentioned edition. I am grateful to Dennis O'Driscoll for providing me with George D. Gopen's helpful prose translation of *Moral Fables* (University of Notre Dame Press/Scottish Academic Press, 1987) at a moment when I might have been inclined to give up on the job. And to Professor Patrick Crotty for his encouragement and informed attention.

This book contains no critical apparatus (the above editions being readily available), but the following points may be of assistance or interest to the non-specialist reader:

'The Prologue': The Latin tag attributed to the legendary Aesop means 'serious subjects are more attractive [have a sweeter smile] when portrayed with a light touch'. The line is actually drawn from one of Henryson's medieval sources.

'The Cock and the Jasp' is included because the conclusion of the prologue requires it, although (as Douglas Gray comments) 'the allegorical interpretation [in the 'Moralitas'] comes as a surprise to most modern readers.' Traditionally, the cock who leaves the jewel in the dirt represents the foolish man who rejects wisdom and constitutes thereby a warning to the reader of the fables to pay attention to their hidden meanings – the kernels in the nuts. But confusion arises here because the cock's reasons for rejecting the jewel are rather praiseworthy and seem to go against the notion of him as a fool.

'The Lion and the Mouse': There is no proof that Aesop, who appears in the dream vision at the opening of this fable, ever existed. He is nevertheless credited with having invented the fable form and having composed the originals upon which all subsequent versions were based. Here his handsome appearance and medieval apparel are at variance with traditional classical accounts of him as an ill-favoured Greek slave of the sixth century BC.

'The Preaching of the Swallow': In the translation of this fable I retain the Scots words 'lint' and 'beets' (meaning flax and bound sheaves of flax) because they have always been part of my own Northern Irish vocabulary.

'The Fox, the Wolf and the Carter': This story involves a play upon words. When the fox has robbed the carter of his herring and escaped, the carter threatens him with a 'nekherring', a word which was not in common use but which occurs, as Denton Fox notes, in *Catholicon Anglicum* (*c*.1475) where it is glossed *colaphus* (in medieval Latin, 'a blow on the neck'). When the carter shouts

> '*Abyde, and thou a nekherring sall haif*
> *Is worth my capill, creillis, and all the laif,*'

the wolf hears the 'herring' bit, the only bit that interests him, and this provides the fox with an opportunity to invent his tale of the luscious 'herring treat'. My solution was to avoid any use of 'nekherring' in my version of the carter's threat and to exploit instead the violence and menace in the word 'gutting', so closely associated with the fish in the creel:

> 'A gutting I'll give you, a herring treat,
> A second helping that you'll not forget.'

This allows the fox (and me, I hope) to play on the words when the wolf asks 'What was that idiot shouting/ When he hunted you and howled and shook his fist?'

THE TESTAMENT OF CRESSEID

ANE DOOLIE SESSOUN to ane cairfull dyte
Suld correspond and be equivalent:
Richt sa it wes quhen I began to wryte
This tragedie – the wedder richt fervent,
Quhen Aries, in middis of the lent,
Schouris of haill gart fra the north discend,
That scant me fra the cauld I micht defend.

Yit nevertheles within myne oratur
I stude, quhen Titan had his bemis bricht
Withdrawin doun and sylit under cure,
And fair Venus, the bewtie of the nicht,
Uprais and set unto the west full richt
Hir goldin face, in oppositioun
Of god Phebus, direct discending doun.

Throwout the glas hir bemis brast sa fair
That I micht se on everie syde me by;
The northin wind had purifyit the air
And sched the mistie cloudis fra the sky;
The froist freisit, the blastis bitterly
Fra Pole Artick come quhisling loud and schill,
And causit me remufe aganis my will.

A GLOOMY TIME, a poem full of hurt
Should correspond and be equivalent.
Just so it was when I began my work
On this retelling, and the weather went
From close to frosty, as Aries, mid-Lent,
Made showers of hail from the north descend
In a great cold I barely could withstand.

Still, there I stood, inside my oratory
When Titan had withdrawn his beams of light
And draped and sealed the brightness of the day,
And lovely Venus, beauty of the night,
Had risen up and toward the true west set
Her golden face, direct in opposition
To the god Phoebus, straight descending down.

Beyond the glass her beams broke out so fair
I could see away on every side of me.
The northern wind had purified the air
And hunted the cloud-cover off the sky.
The frost froze hard, the blast came bitterly
From the pole-star, whistling loud and shrill,
And forced me to remove against my will.

For I traistit that Venus, luifis quene,
To quhome sum tyme I hecht obedience,
My faidit hart of lufe scho wald mak grene,
And therupon with humbill reverence
I thocht to pray hir hie magnificence;
Bot for greit cald as than I lattit was,
And in my chalmer to the fyre can pas.

Thocht lufe be hait, yit in ane man of age
It kendillis nocht sa sone as in youtheid,
Of quhome the blude is flowing in ane rage;
And in the auld the curage doif and deid,
Of quhilk the fyre outward is best remeid:
To help be phisike quhair that nature faillit
I am expert, for baith I have assaillit.

I mend the fyre and beikit me about,
Than tuik ane drink, my spreitis to comfort,
And armit me weill fra the cauld thairout.
To cut the winter nicht and mak it schort
I tuik ane quair – and left all uther sport –
Writtin be worthie Chaucer glorious,
Of fair Creisseid and worthie Troylus.

And thair I fand, efter that Diomeid
Ressavit had that lady bricht of hew,
How Troilus neir out of wit abraid
And weipit soir with visage paill of hew;
For quhilk wanhope his teiris can renew,
Quhill esperance rejoisit him agane:
Thus quhyle in joy he levit, quhyle in pane.

I had placed my trust in Venus, as love's queen
To whom one time I vowed obedience,
That she should sprig my fallow heart with green;
And there and then, with humble reverence,
I thought to pray her high magnificence,
But hindered by that freezing arctic air
Returned into my chamber to the fire.

Though love is hot, yet in an older man
It kindles not so soon as in the young:
Their blood burns furiously in every vein
But in the old the blaze is lapsed so long
It needs an outer fire to burn and bring
The spark to life – as I myself know well:
Remedies, when the urge dies, can avail.

I stacked the fire and got warm at the hearth,
Then took a drink to soothe and lift my spirit
And arm myself against the bitter north.
To pass the time and kill the winter night
I chose a book – and was soon absorbed in it –
Written by Chaucer, the great and glorious,
About fair Cresseid and worthy Troilus.

And there I found that after Diomede
Had won that lady in her radiance
Troilus was driven nearly mad
And wept sore and lost colour and then, once
He had despaired his fill, would recommence
As memory and hope revived again.
Thus whiles he lived in joy and whiles in pain.

Of hir behest he had greit comforting,
Traisting to Troy that scho suld mak retour,
Quhilk he desyrit maist of eirdly thing,
Forquhy scho was his only paramour.
Bot quhen he saw passit baith day and hour
Of hir ganecome, than sorrow can oppres
His wofull hart in cair and hevines.

Of his distres me neidis nocht reheirs,
For worthie Chauceir in the samin buik,
In gudelie termis and in joly veirs,
Compylit hes his cairis, quha will luik.
To brek my sleip ane uther quair I tuik,
In quhilk I fand the fatall destenie
Of fair Cresseid, that endit wretchitlie.

Quha wait gif all that Chauceir wrait was trew?
Nor I wait nocht gif this narratioun
Be authoreist, or fenyeit of the new
Be sum poeit, throw his inventioun
Maid to report the lamentatioun
And wofull end of this lustie Creisseid,
And quhat distres scho thoillit, and quhat deid.

Quhen Diomeid had all his appetyte,
And mair, fulfillit of this fair ladie,
Upon ane uther he set his haill delyte,
And send to hir ane lybell of repudie,
And hir excludit fra his companie.
Than desolait scho walkit up and doun,
And sum men sayis, into the court, commoun.

She had promised him and this was his consoling.
He trusted her to come to Troy once more
Which he desired more than any thing
Because she was his only paramour.
But when he saw the day and the due hour
Of her return go past, a heavy weight
Of care and woe oppressed his broken heart.

No need here to rehearse the man's distress
Since worthy Chaucer in that selfsame book
Has told his troubles in beguiling verse
And pleasant style, whoever cares to look.
It was a different volume that I took
To keep myself awake, in which I found
Cresseid's most miserable and fated end.

Who knows if all that Chaucer wrote was true?
Nor do I know if this second version
Was genuine, or maybe something new
Invented by a poet, some narration
Framed so as to include the lamentation
And woeful fall of passionate Cresseid,
What she would endure and how she died.

When Diomede had sated his desire
And oversated it on this fair lady
He sought fresh satisfactions with another
And sent Cresseid a banishment decree
To bind and bar her from his company.
She went distracted then and would ramble
And be, as men will say, available.

O fair Creisseid, the flour and A per se
Of Troy and Grece, how was thow fortunait
To change in filth all thy feminitie,
And be with fleschelie lust sa maculait,
And go amang the Greikis air and lait,
Sa giglotlike takand thy foull plesance!
I have pietie thow suld fall sic mischance!

Yit nevertheless, quhat ever men deme or say
In scornefull langage of thy brukkilnes,
I sall excuse als far furth as I may
Thy womanheid, thy wisdome and fairnes,
The quhilk fortoun hes put to sic distres
As hir pleisit, and nathing throw the gilt
Of the, throw wickit langage to be spilt!

This fair lady, in this wyse destitute
Of all comfort and consolatioun,
Richt privelie, but fellowschip or refute,
Disagysit passit far out of the toun
Ane myle or twa, unto ane mansioun
Beildit full gay, quhair hir father Calchas
Quhilk than amang the Greikis dwelland was.

Quhen he hir saw, the caus he can inquyre
Of hir cumming; scho said, siching full soir,
'Fra Diomeid had gottin his desyre
He wox werie and wald of me no moir.'
Quod Calchas, 'Douchter, weip thow not thairfoir;
Peraventure all cummis for the best.
Welcum to me; thow art full deir ane gest!'

O fair Cresseid, the flower and paragon
Of Troy and Greece, how could it be your fate
To let yourself be dragged down as a woman
And sullied so by lustful appetite
To go among the Greeks early and late
So obviously, like any common pickup?
When I recollect your fall, I want to weep.

And yet whatever men may think or say
Contemptuously about your quick compliance
I will excuse to what extent I may
Your womanhood, wisdom and loveliness
Which the whim of fortune put to such distress –
No guilt for it to be attributed
To you, bad-mouthed by noxious gossip.

Then fair Cresseid, completely destitute,
Bereft of comfort and all consolation,
Friendless and unprotected, managed out
By stealth and in disguise beyond the town
A mile or two and crossed beyond the line
To a splendid mansion in the Greek-held quarter,
The residence of Calchas, her old father.

When he saw her there, he enquired why
She had returned. 'From the moment Diomede
Had his pleasure,' she answered desperately,
'He began to tire of me and have no need.'
'There is nothing here to weep for,' Calchas said,
'It could be all has turned out for the best.
You are welcome, daughter dear, my dearest guest.'

This auld Calchas, efter the law was tho,
Wes keiper of the tempill as ane preist
In quhilk Venus and hir sone Cupido
War honourit, and his chalmer was thame neist;
To quhilk Cresseid, with baill aneuch in breist,
Usit to pas, hir prayeris for to say,
Quhill at the last, upon ane solempne day,

As custome was, the pepill far and neir
Befoir the none unto the tempill went
With sacrifice, devoit in thair maneir;
Bot still Cresseid, hevie in hir intent,
Into the kirk wald not hir self present,
For giving of the pepill ony deming
Of hir expuls fra Diomeid the king;

Bot past into ane secreit orature,
Quhair scho micht weip hir wofull desteny.
Behind hir bak scho cloisit fast the dure
And on hir kneis bair fell doun in hy;
Upon Venus and Cupide angerly
Scho cryit out, and said on this same wyse:
'Allace, that ever I maid yow sacrifice!

'Ye gave me anis ane devine responsaill
That I suld be the flour of luif in Troy;
Now am I maid ane unworthie outwaill,
And all in cair translatit is my joy.
Quha sall me gyde? Quha sall me now convoy,
Sen I fra Diomeid and nobill Troylus
Am clene excludit, as abject odious?

Old Calchas, as the law required then
Of temple-keepers, was a temple-priest,
Servant of Venus and Cupid, her young son,
Keeper of their precincts where, distressed,
Cresseid would go, heart heavy in her breast,
To hide from public notice and to pray.
And then it happened on a certain day

When custom called for general devotion
And sacrifice was due, the people went
Devoutly to the temple before noon;
But still Cresseid stayed firm in her intent
To avoid the sanctuary and not present
Herself in public, to keep her secret safe,
Not let them guess her prince had cast her off.

She moved instead into a cell, in private,
Where she might weep for what had come to pass.
Behind her back she closed the door and barred it,
Then hurriedly fell down on her bare knees,
Crying all the while, berating Venus
And Cupid angrily, in words like these:
'Why, alas, did I ever sacrifice

To you, you gods, who once divinely promised
That I would be the flower of love in Troy?
I have been demeaned into an outcast,
Translated and betrayed out of my joy.
Who's now to guide, accompany or stand by
Me, set at odds and made so odious
To Diomede and noble Troilus?

'O fals Cupide, is nane to wyte bot thow
And thy mother, of lufe the blind goddes!
Ye causit me alwayis understand and trow
The seid of lufe was sawin in my face,
And ay grew grene throw your supplie and grace.
Bot now, allace, that seid with froist is slane,
And I fra luifferis left, and all forlane.'

Quhen this was said, doun in ane extasie,
Ravischit in spreit, intill ane dreame scho fell,
And be apperance hard, quhair scho did ly,
Cupide the king ringand ane silver bell,
Quhilk men micht heir fra hevin unto hell;
At quhais sound befoir Cupide appeiris
The sevin planetis, discending fra thair spheiris;

Quhilk hes power of all thing generabill,
To reull and steir be thair greit influence
Wedder and wind, and coursis variabill.
And first of all Saturne gave his sentence,
Quhilk gave to Cupide litill reverence,
Bot as ane busteous churle on his maneir
Come crabitlie with auster luik and cheir.

His face fronsit, his lyre was lyke the leid,
His teith chatterit and cheverit with the chin,
His ene drowpit, how sonkin in his heid,
Out of his nois the meldrop fast can rin,
With lippis bla and cheikis leine and thin;
The ice-schoklis that fra his hair doun hang
Was wonder greit, and as ane speir als lang.

O false Cupid, none is to blame but you,
You and your mother, who is love's blind goddess.
You gave me to believe and I trusted you
That the seed of love was sown in my face
And would grow greener through your constant grace.
But now, alas, that seed with frost is killed
And I from lovers banished forth and exiled.'

When this was said, her spirits ebbed away
In a fainting fit and into dream she fell
So that it seemed she heard from where she lay
Cupid the King ringing a silver bell
That filled men's ears from heaven down to hell.
At which sound before Cupid there appear
The seven planets, descending from their spheres.

They of all things brought into creation
Have power to rule through their great influence
Wind and weather and the course of fortune,
And Saturn, being first up to pronounce,
Treated Cupid with no great reverence
But crabbedly, with cramped look and demeanour,
Behaved in his churlish, rough, thick-witted manner.

With rucked and wrinkled face, a lyre like lead,
His chattering teeth sent shivers through his chin,
His eyes were droopy, holes sunk in his head,
His lips were blue, his cheek hollow and thin,
And from his nose there streamed a steady nose-run.
And lo too, and behold! Down from his hair
Hung icicles as long as any spear.

Atovir his belt his lyart lokkis lay
Felterit unfair, ovirfret with froistis hoir,
His garmound and his gyte full gay of gray,
His widderit weid fra him the wind out woir,
Ane busteous bow within his hand he boir,
Under his girdill ane flasche of felloun flanis
Fedderit with ice and heidit with hailstanis.

Than Juppiter, richt fair and amiabill,
God of the starnis in the firmament
And nureis to all thing generabill;
Fra his father Saturne far different,
With burelie face and browis bricht and brent;
Upon his heid ane garland wonder gay
Of flouris fair, as it had bene in May.

His voice was cleir, as cristall wer his ene,
As goldin wyre sa glitterand was his hair,
His garmound and his gyte full gay of grene
With goldin listis gilt on everie gair;
Ane burelie brand about his middill bair,
In his richt hand he had ane groundin speir,
Of his father the wraith fra us to weir.

Nixt efter him come Mars the god of ire,
Of strife, debait, and all dissensioun,
To chide and fecht, als feirs as ony fyre,
In hard harnes, hewmound, and habirgeoun,
And on his hanche ane roustie fell fachioun,
And in his hand he had ane roustie sword,
Wrything his face with mony angrie word.

Around his belt, his hoary lank locks lay
Tousled and messed and tinselled with the frost.
His cloak and suit were of a gloomy grey,
Like faded flags they flapped on him and tossed.
He held a hefty bow in his strong grasp,
A sheaf of cruel arrows in his sash
With hailstone heads and feather-flights of ice.

Then Jupiter, so amiable, so handsome,
God of all stars in the firmament
And nurse of all potential and creation,
The son of Saturn but far different:
Fine-featured face, his forehead radiant,
A garland on his head, a lovely spray
Woven of flowers that made it seem like May.

His voice was clear, his crystal eyes were keen,
His fair hair had the shine of golden wire,
His cloak and suit were of a glorious green
With gilt appliqué hems on every gore.
A gallant sword strapped to his waist he wore
And in his right hand held a sharpened spear
To keep us safe and ward off Saturn's anger.

Next after him came Mars, the god of ire,
Of strife and of debate and all dissension,
To quarrel and attack as quick as wildfire,
In armour dressed, helmet and habergeon.
He flaunted at his hip a dangerous falchion
As rusty as the sword he held aloft,
And raged, grimaced, rampaged and bawled and scoffed.

Schaikand his sword, befoir Cupide he come,
With reid visage and grislie glowrand ene,
And at his mouth ane bullar stude of fome,
Lyke to ane bair quhetting his tuskis kene;
Richt tuilyeour lyke, but temperance in tene,
Ane horne he blew with mony bosteous brag,
Quhilk all this warld with weir hes maid to wag.

Than fair Phebus, lanterne and lamp of licht,
Of man and beist, baith frute and flourisching,
Tender nureis, and banischer of nicht,
And of the warld causing, be his moving
And influence, lyfe in all eirdlie thing,
Without comfort of quhome, of force, to nocht
Must all ga die that in this warld is wrocht.

As king royall he raid upon his chair,
The quhilk Phaeton gydit sum tyme unricht;
The brichtnes of his face quhen it was bair
Nane micht behald for peirsing of his sicht;
This goldin cart with fyrie bemis bricht
Four yokkit steidis full different of hew
But bait or tyring throw the spheiris drew.

The first was soyr, with mane als reid as rois,
Callit Eoye, into the orient;
The secund steid to name hecht Ethios,
Quhitlie and paill, and sum deill ascendent;
The thrid Peros, richt hait and richt fervent;
The feird was blak, and callit Philogie,
Quhilk rollis Phebus doun into the sey.

Shaking this sword, before Cupid he comes,
Red in the face and glowering balefully.
Like a boar that whets its tusks, he grinds and fumes
And foams at the mouth, making spittle fly.
Brawling, spoiling, keeping himself angry,
He blows coarse, constant blasts upon a horn
That has rocked this world with war to its foundation.

Then Phoebus fair, lantern and lamp of light,
Tender nurse of flourishing and fruiting,
Of man and beast; the banisher of night;
By influence and motion cause and spring
Of life in the world and every earthly thing;
Without whose comfort, all that has been brought
Into being needs must die and count for naught.

As king in state, he rode his chariot,
The one that Phaeton had once driven off course.
The brightness of his countenance when not
Shielded would hurt the eyes of onlookers.
The golden coach, with its gleaming fiery rays,
Four harnessed steeds, each differently coloured,
Drew through the spheres and never slowed or tired.

The first was sorrel, his mane red as a rose,
Eous his name, the east his element.
The second was the steed called Ethios,
Whitish and pale, inclined to the ascendant.
The third was Peros, hot-blooded and ardent.
The fourth, a black steed named Philogeus,
Rolls Phoebus down into the western seas.

Venus was thair present, that goddes gay,
Hir sonnis querrell for to defend, and mak
Hir awin complaint, cled in ane nyce array,
The ane half grene, the uther half sabill blak,
Quhyte hair as gold, kemmit and sched abak;
Bot in hir face semit greit variance,
Quhyles perfyte treuth and quhyles inconstance.

Under smyling scho was dissimulait,
Provocative with blenkis amorous,
And suddanely changit and alterait,
Angrie as ony serpent vennemous,
Richt pungitive with wordis odious;
Thus variant scho was, quha list tak keip:
With ane eye lauch, and with the uther weip,

In taikning that all fleschelie paramour,
Quhilk Venus hes in reull and governance,
I sum tyme sweit, sum tyme bitter and sour,
Richt unstabill and full of variance,
Mingit with cairfull joy and fals plesance,
Now hait, now cauld, now blyith, now full of wo,
Now grene as leif, now widderit and ago.

With buik in hand than come Mercurius,
Richt eloquent and full of rethorie,
With polite termis and delicious,
With pen and ink to report all reddie,
Setting sangis and singand merilie;
His hude was reid, heklit atovir his croun,
Lyke to ane poeit of the auld fassoun.

Venus attended too, that lovely goddess,
There to plead her son's case, and to make
Her own complaint, dressed with a certain feyness,
Half of her costume green, half sable black,
Her golden hair combed, parted and drawn back;
But in her face great variance seemed to be,
Inconstant now, now faithful absolutely.

For all her smiling, she was a deceiver.
Her insinuating becks and glances
Could change all of a sudden and reveal her
Serpent anger, in the spit and hiss
Of language that was truly venomous.
Her changeableness was there for all to see:
A tear in one, a smile in the other eye.

Betokening this: that bodily desire
Which Venus has it in her power to rule
Is sweet at times, at times bitter and sour,
Unstable always, ever variable,
Its pleasures sad, joys unreliable,
Now hot, now cold, now blithe, now full of woe,
Now green in leaf, now withered on the bough.

Then, with his book in hand, came Mercury,
So eloquent, adept in rhetoric,
With stylish terms and sweet delivery,
Ready to record in pen and ink,
Composing, singing, setting tune and lyric.
His hood was red, a thing of frills and scallops
Worn above his crown like an old-time poet's.

Boxis he bair with fyne electuairis,
And sugerit syropis for digestioun,
Spycis belangand to the pothecairis,
With mony hailsum sweit confectioun;
Doctour in phisick, cled in ane skarlot goun,
And furrit weill – as sic ane aucht to be –
Honest and gude, and not ane word culd lie.

Nixt efter him come lady Cynthia,
The last of all and swiftest in hir spheir;
Of colour blak, buskit with hornis twa,
And in the nicht scho listis best appeir;
Haw as the leid, of colour nathing cleir,
For all hir licht scho borrowis at hir brother
Titan, for of hirself scho hes nane uther.

Hir gyte was gray and full of spottis blak,
And on hir breist ane churle paintit full evin
Beirand ane bunche of thornis on his bak,
Quhilk for his thift micht clim na nar the hevin.
Thus quhen thay gadderit war, thir goddes sevin,
Mercurius thay cheisit with ane assent
To be foirspeikar in the parliament.

Quha had bene thair and liken for to heir
His facound toung and termis exquisite,
Of rethorick the prettick he micht leir,
In breif sermone ane pregnant sentence wryte.
Befoir Cupide veiling his cap a-lyte,
Speiris the caus of that vocatioun,
And he anone schew his intentioun.

Boxes he bore with fine electuaries
And sugared syrups, aids for the digestion,
Spices belonging to apothecaries
And many other wholesome sweet confections.
Clad in scarlet, doctor of medicine,
Gowned and well furred – as such a one should be –
A good and honest man who did not lie.

Next after him came Lady Cynthia,
Last of all and swiftest in her sphere,
Darkling and in double-horned regalia
As in the night she likes best to appear –
Blue-grey like lead, a colour that's unclear
Since all her light she borrows from her brother
Titan, her single source. She has no other.

Her gown was grey with patterned spots of black
And on her breast a painting of a peasant
Bearing a bunch of thorn sticks on his back,
The theft of which still foiled his climb to heaven.
And so from among themselves, that group of seven
Gods chose Mercury with one assent
To be the spokesman in their parliament.

Whoever had been there and interested
To hear his speech, so well turned and precise,
Would have learnt the art of rhetoric, how to put
A weighty meaning in a brief address.
Doffing his cap to Cupid, he requests
To know why they'd been summoned there in session
And Cupid promptly made his accusation.

'Lo,' quod Cupide, 'quha will blaspheme the name
Of his awin god, outher in word or deid,
To all goddis he dois baith lak and schame,
And suld have bitter panis to his meid;
I say this by yone wretchit Cresseid,
The quhilk throw me was sum tyme flour of lufe,
Me and my mother starklie can reprufe,

'Saying of hir greit infelicitie
I was the caus, and my mother Venus,
Ane blind goddes hir cald, that micht not se,
With sclander and defame injurious.
Thus hir leving unclene and lecherous
Scho wald retorte in me and my mother,
To quhome I schew my grace alone all uther.

'And sen ye ar all sevin deificait,
Participant of devyne sapience,
This greit injure done to our hie estait
Me think with pane we suld mak recompence;
Was never to goddes done sic violence.
As weill for yow as for myself I say:
Thairfoir ga help to revenge, I yow pray!'

Mercurius to Cupide gave answeir
And said, 'Schir King, my counsall is that ye
Refer yow to the hiest planeit heir
And tak to him the lawest of degré,
The pane of Cresseid for to modifie –
As God Saturne, with him tak Cynthia.'
'I am content', quod he, 'to tak thay twa.'

'Whoever', he began, 'blasphemes the name
Of his own god, in either word or deed,
To all gods offers insult and brings shame
And deserves hard punishment upon that head.
I say this because yon miserable Cresseid
Who thanks to me was once the flower of love
Offered me and my mother stark reproof,

Saying I was the cause of her misfortune;
And furthermore she called my mother Venus
A blind goddess, thus slandering love's queen
In terms defaming and injurious.
So for her life unchaste and lecherous
She whom I favoured more than any other
Would lay the blame on me and on my mother.

And since you seven all participate
In power divine and knowledge, you are owed
Due recompense; the slight to your estate
Should be, I think, most painfully repaid.
There never was such violence done to gods.
So as much for you as for myself I say,
Come lend a hand: revenge! That is my plea.'

Mercury answered Cupid, 'Royal sir,
This counsel I would give your majesty:
Rest your case with the highest planet here.
Let him, with her who's lowest in degree,
Decide how painful Cresseid's fate should be –
Saturn and Lady Cynthia, I mean.'
'I am content,' he said, 'I agree to them.'

Than thus proceidit Saturne and the Mone
Quhen thay the mater rypelie had degest:
For the dispyte to Cupide scho had done
And to Venus, oppin and manifest,
In all hir lyfe with pane to be opprest,
And torment sair with seiknes incurabill,
And to all lovers be abhominabill.

This duleful sentence Saturne tuik on hand,
And passit doun quhair cairfull Cresseid lay,
And on hir heid he laid ane frostie wand.
Than lawfullie on this wyse can he say:
'Thy greit fairnes and all thy bewtie gay,
Thy wantoun blude, and eik thy goldin hair,
Heir I exclude fra the for evermair.

'I change thy mirth into melancholy,
Quhilk is the mother of all pensivenes;
Thy moisture and thy heit in cald and dry;
Thyne insolence, thy play and wantones
To greit diseis; thy pomp and thy riches
In mortall neid; and greit penuritie
Thow suffer sall, and as ane beggar die.'

O cruell Saturne, fraward and angrie,
Hard is thy dome and to malitious!
On fair Cresseid quhy hes thow na mercie,
Quhilk was sa sweit, gentill and amorous?
Withdraw thy sentence and be gracious –
As thow was never; sa schawis throw thy deid,
Ane wraikfull sentence gevin on fair Cresseid.

Thus they passed sentence, Saturn and the Moon,
After due process of deliberation:
Since the injury that Cresseid had done
Cupid and Venus was manifest and blatant
She would live in painful torment from then on,
By lovers be despised, abominable,
Beyond the pale, diseased, incurable.

This grievous sentence Saturn took charge of,
And coming down to where sad Cresseid lay
He placed upon her head a frosty tipstaff
And spoke as follows in his legal way:
'Your great good looks and your delightful beauty,
Your hot blood and your golden hair also
Henceforth forevermore I disallow you.

Your mirth I hereby change to melancholy
Which is the mother of all downcastness,
Your moisture and your heat to cold and dry,
Your lust, presumption and your giddiness
To great disease; your pomp and show and riches
To fatal need; and you will suffer
Penury extreme and die a beggar.'

O cruel Saturn, ill-natured and angry,
Your doom is hard and too malicious.
Why to fair Cresseid won't you show mercy
Who was so loving, kind and courteous?
Withdraw your sentence and be gracious –
Who never have been: it shows in what you did,
A vengeful sentence passed on fair Cresseid.

Than Cynthia, quhen Saturne past away,
Out of hir sait discendit doun belyve,
And red ane bill on Cresseid quhair scho lay,
Contening this sentence diffinityve:
'Fra heit of bodie I the now depryve,
And to thy seiknes sall be na recure
Bot in dolour thy dayis to indure.

'Thy cristall ene minglit with blude I mak,
Thy voice sa cleir, unplesand, hoir and hace,
Thy lustie lyre ovirspred with spottis blak,
And lumpis haw appeirand in thy face:
Quhair thow cummis, ilk man sall fle the place.
This sall thow go begging fra hous to hous
With cop and clapper lyke ane lazarous.'

This doolie dreame, this uglye visioun
Brocht to ane end, Cresseid fra it awoik,
And all that court and convocatioun
Vanischit away. Than rais scho up and tuik
Ane poleist glas, and hir schaddow culd luik;
And quhen scho saw hir face sa deformait,
Gif scho in hart was wa aneuch, God wait!

Weiping full sair, 'Lo, quhat it is', quod sche,
'With fraward langage for to mufe and steir
Our craibit goddis; and sa is sene on me!
My blaspheming now have I bocht full deir;
All eirdlie joy and mirth I set areir.
Allace, this day! allace, this wofull tyde
Quhen I began with my goddis for to chyde!'

Then Cynthia, when Saturn moved away,
Left her seat and descended down below
And read decrees on Cresseid where she lay
Spelling out the last word of the law:
'I hereby of your body's heat deprive you
And for your sickness there shall be no cure,
Your days to come days solely to endure.

Your eyes so bright and crystal I make bloodshot,
Your voice so clear, unpleasing, grating, hoarse.
Your healthy skin I blacken, blotch and spot.
With livid lumps I cover your fair face.
Go where you will, all men will flee the place.
From house to house you'll travel thus, a leper
Begging your way, bearing a cup and clapper.'

When this dark dream, this terrifying vision
Concluded, Cresseid, released, awoke
And all that sitting court and convocation
Vanished away. Then up she rose and took
A polished looking glass where she could look
And when she saw her face in it so ruined
God knows if she was not heartsore and stunned.

Bitterly weeping, 'Lo, what it means', said she,
'To contradict and aggravate and rouse
Our ill-set gods. Look and take note of me.
My blasphemy is paid for now, alas.
I leave behind all earthly happiness.
Alas the day! Alas the time and tide
I ever remonstrated with a god!'

Be this was said, ane chyld come fra the hall
To warne Cresseid the supper was reddy;
First knokkit at the dure, and syne culd call,
'Madame, your father biddis yow cum in hy:
He hes merwell sa lang on grouf ye ly,
And sayis your beedes bene to lang sum deill;
The goddis wait all your intent full weill.'

Quod scho, 'Fair chyld, ga to my father deir,
And pray him cum to speik with me anone.'
And sa he did, and said, 'Douchter, quhat cheir?'
'Allace!' quod scho, 'Father, my mirth is gone!'
'How sa?' quod he; and scho can all expone,
As I have tauld, the vengeance and the wraik
For hir trespas Cupide on hir culd tak.

He luikit on hir uglye lipper face,
The quhylk befor was quhite as lillie flour;
Wringand his handis, oftymes he said, allace
That he had levit to se that wofull hour!
For he knew weill that thair was na succour
To hir seiknes, and that dowblit his pane;
Thus was thair cair aneuch betuix thame twane.

Quhen thay togidder murnit had full lang,
Quod Cresseid: 'Father, I wald not be kend;
Thairfoir in secreit wyse ye let me gang
Unto yone spitall at the tounis end,
And thidder sum meit for cheritie me send
To leif upon, for all mirth in this eird
Is fra me gane – sic is my wickit weird!'

When this was said, a child came from the hall
To notify Cresseid supper awaited.
He knocked first at the door, then gave the call:
'Madam, make haste. Your father bids. You're needed.
He is amazed you lie so long prostrated.
He says you spend too long at your devotions,
That the gods well know your prayers and petitions.'

'Fair child,' she said, 'go to my father dear
And pray him come to speak with me anon.'
And so he did and 'Daughter,' exclaimed, 'what cheer?'
'Father,' she cried, 'alas, my mirth is gone!'
'How so?' he asked, and she told there and then
What I have told, the vengeance and redress
Cupid had exacted for her trespass.

He looked upon her ugly leprous face,
Fair until then as any lily flower.
Wringing his hands, he cried and cried alas
That he had lived to see that woeful hour
For well he knew that there would be no cure
For her disease, which doubled his own grief.
And so between them there was pain enough.

Together they lamented long, and then
'Father,' said Cresseid, 'I cannot bear
To be recognised, so let me go unknown
To yon leper house beyond the town, and there
Keep me in food and charitable care
And I will live. All happiness on earth
Has left me now, I take my fated path.'

Than in ane mantill and ane baver hat,
With cop and clapper, wonder prively,
He opnit ane secreit yet, and out thairat
Convoyit hir, that na man suld espy,
Unto ane village half ane myle thairby;
Delyverit hir in at the spittaill hous,
And daylie sent hir part of his almous.

Sum knew hir weill, and sum had na knawledge
Of hir becaus scho was sa deformait,
With bylis blak ovirspred in hir visage,
And hir fair colour faidit and alterait.
Yit thay presumit, for hir hie regrait
And still murning, scho was of nobill kin;
With better will thairfoir they tuik hir in.

The day passit and Phebus went to rest,
The cloudis blak overheled all the sky.
God wait gif Cresseid was ane sorrowfull gest,
Seing that uncouth fair and harbery!
But meit or drink scho dressit hir to ly
In ane dark corner of the hous allone,
And on this wyse, weiping, scho maid hir mone:

'O sop of sorrow, sonkin into cair!
O cative Creisseid! For now and ever mair
Gane is thy joy and all thy mirth in eird;
Of all blyithnes now art thou blaiknit bair;
Thair is na salve may saif or sound thy sair!
Fell is thy fortoun, wickit is thy weird,
Thy blys is baneist, and thy baill on breird!

For her then, in her cloak and beaver hat,
With cup and clapper, very stealthily
He opened secret gates and let her out,
Conveying her unseen by anybody
To a village about half a mile away;
Left her there in the leper colony
And sent in victuals to her every day.

Some knew her well, and others not at all
Because of her appearance, so deformed,
Her face all covered over with black boils,
Her colour pale, her lovely skin ringwormed.
Still, they assumed from grief so mildly borne
And yet so cruel, she was of noble kin
And with better will, therefore, they took her in.

The daylight died and Phoebus went to rest.
Black nightclouds spread out over the whole sky.
Cresseid, God knows, must have been a stricken guest
As she viewed her plate and pallet in dismay.
Eat or drink she would not, but made ready
For bed in a dark corner where she went
To weep alone, and utter this lament.

CRESSEID'S LAMENT

'O sop of sorrow, sunk and steeped in care!
O poor Cresseid! Now and for evermore
Delight on earth is gone, and all your joy.
There is no salve can heal or soothe your sore.
Your spirit flags that was flushed up before.
Your fate will doom you, destiny destroy.
Your bliss is banished and fresh fears annoy.

Under the eirth, God gif I gravin wer,
Quhair nane of Grece nor yit of Troy micht heird!

'*Quhair is thy chalmer wantounlie besene,*
With burely bed and bankouris browderit bene?
Spycis and wyne to thy collatioun,
The cowpis all of gold and silver schene,
The sweitmeitis servit in plaittis clene
With saipheron sals of ane gude sessoun?
Thy gay garmentis with mony gudely goun,
Thy plesand lawn pinnit with goldin prene?
All is areir, thy greit royall renoun!

'*Quhair is thy garding with thir greissis gay*
And fresche flowris, quhilk the quene Floray
Had paintit plesandly in everie pane,
Quhair thou was wont full merilye in May
To walk and tak the dew be it was day,
And heir the merle and mawis mony ane,
With ladyis fair in carrolling to gane,
And se the royall rinkis in thair ray,
In garmentis gay garnischit on everie grane?

'*Thy greit triumphand fame and hie honour,*
Quhair thou was callit of eirdlye wichtis flour,
All is decayit, thy weird is welterit so;
Thy hie estait is turnit in darknes dour;
This lipper ludge tak for thy burelie bour,
And for thy bed tak now ane bunche of stro,
For waillit wyne and meitis thou had tho
Tak mowlit breid, peirrie and ceder sour:
Bot cop and clapper now is all ago.

God send me under earth, down through death's door
Where no one's heard the name of Greece or Troy.

'Where is your chamber's cushioned chair and screen
And handsome bed and hand-embroidered linen?
The wine and spice, the supper that you supped on?
Where are the cups of gold and silver sheen,
The sweetmeats and the saffron sauce, the clean
Platters they were seasoned and served up on?
Your goodly raiment and many a stately gown,
Your shawl of lawn pinned up with its gold pin?
It's as if it never was, your high renown.

'Where is your garden full of herb and spray
And Flora's flowers, which she so pleasantly
Planted in every cranny where they sprang,
And where most blithely in the month of May
You'd walk and wade the dew at break of day
And hear the thrush and blackbird at their song
And go with ladies, carolling along,
And see the knights beribboned *cap-à-pie,*
Arrayed in ranks to crowd the royal throng.

'Your name and fame that held the world in thrall,
Your triumphs there, the flower among them all,
Fate overturned. Those days won't come again.
Your high estate is in decline and fall
So make this leper's hut your banquet hall
And make your bed up now in this straw pen.
For the choice wines and dishes you had then
Take mouldy bread, sour cider and pear-gall.
Make do with cup and clapper. They remain.

'My cleir voice and courtlie carrolling,
Quhair I was wont with ladyis for to sing,
Is rawk as ruik, full hiddeous, hoir and hace;
My plesand port, all utheris precelling,
Of lustines I was hald maist conding –
Now is deformit the figour of my face;
To luik on it na leid now lyking hes.
Sowpit in syte, I say with sair siching,
Ludgeit amang the lipper leid, "Allace!"

'O ladyis fair of Troy and Grece, attend
My miserie, quhilk nane may comprehend,
My frivoll fortoun, my infelicitie,
My greit mischief, quhilk na man can amend.
Be war in tyme, approchis neir the end,
And in your mynd ane mirrour mak of me:
As I am now, peradventure that ye
For all your micht may cum to that same end,
Or ellis war, gif ony war may be.

'Nocht is your fairnes bot ane faiding flour,
Nocht is your famous laud and hie honour
Bot wind inflat in uther mennis eiris;
Your roising reid to rotting sall retour;
Exempill mak of me in your memour,
Quhilk of sic thingis wofull witnes beiris.
All welth in eird, away as wind it weiris;
Be war thairfoir, approchis neir the hour:
Fortoun is fikkill quhen scho beginnis and steiris!'

'My voice once clear from courtly carolling
With ladies whom I used to meet to sing
Is like a rook's, grown husky, hoarse and raucous.
I who once moved attractively, excelling
And acknowledged in my beauty, now must hang
My head and turn aside my deformed face.
Nobody wants to see my changed appearance.
Lodged among leper folk, in grief past telling,
I sigh a sore and desolate, Alas!

'O ladies fair of Troy and Greece, attend
To my sad state which none may comprehend,
My fickle fortune, lost felicity,
My great distress that no man may amend.
Beware in time, the end draws close, attend
And in your mind a mirror make of me.
Remember well what I am now, for ye
For all your strength may come to the same end
Or worse again, if any worse may be.

'Your beauty's nothing but a flower that fades,
Nothing your honoured name and famous praise
But mouthfuls of air in other people's ears.
The rot will fester in your cheek's red rose.
Remember and take cognisance: my woes
Bear witness to a world that's full of tears.
All wealth on earth is wind that flits and veers;
Beware therefore in time. The hour draws close
And fate is fickle when she plies the shears.'

Thus chydand with hir drerie destenye,
Weiping scho woik the nicht fra end to end;
Bot all in vane – hir dule, hir cairfull cry,
Micht not remeid nor yit hir murning mend.
Ane lipper lady rais and till hir wend,
And said: 'Quhy spurnis thow aganis the wall
To sla thyself and mend nathing at all?

'Sen thy weiping dowbillis bot thy wo,
I counsall the mak vertew of ane neid;
Go leir to clap thy clapper to and fro,
And leif efter the law of lipper leid.'
Thair was na buit, bot furth with thame scho yeid
Fra place to place, quhill cauld and hounger sair
Compellit hir to be ane rank beggair.

That samin tyme, of Troy the garnisoun,
Quhilk had to chiftane worthie Troylus,
Throw jeopardie of weir had strikken doun
Knichtis of Grece in number mervellous;
With greit tryumphe and laude victorious
Agane to Troy richt royallie thay raid
The way quhair Cresseid with the lipper baid.

Seing that companie, all with ane stevin
Thay gaif ane cry, and schuik coppis gude speid;
Said: 'Worthie lordis, for Goddis lufe of hevin,
To us lipper part of your almous deid!'
Than to thair cry nobill Troylus tuik heid,
Having pietie, neir by the place can pas
Quhair Cresseid sat, not witting quhat scho was.

And so she pleaded her sad destiny
And couldn't sleep for weeping out the night,
But all in vain – her grief and painful cry
Could neither remedy nor mend her plight.
A leper woman rose, went to her side
And 'Why', she said, 'do you kick against the wall
To destroy yourself and do no good at all?

'Your weeping only doubles all you suffer.
Make virtue of necessity. For my sake,
Go and learn to wave and clap your clapper
And live the life required of leper folk.'
There was no help, so out with them she took
Her way from place to place, till cold and hunger
Compelled her to become an utter beggar.

At that same time the garrison of Troy
Led by their chieftain, worthy Troilus,
Had beaten down, by war and jeopardy,
The Grecian knights. The rout was marvellous
So back to Troy, triumphant, glorious
In victory, right royally they rode
Past where Cresseid with lepers made abode.

Seeing that company, they cried as one
And shook their cups immediately and prayed,
'Good lords, for the love of God in heaven,
Spare us your alms, our lepers' livelihood.'
Then noble Troilus to their cry paid heed
And pitied them and passed by near the place
Where Cresseid sat, not knowing who she was.

Than upon him scho kest up baith hir ene –
And with ane blenk it come into his thocht
That he sumtime hir face befoir had sene.
Bot scho was in sic plye he knew hir nocht;
Yit than hir luik into his mynd it brocht
The sweit visage and amorous blenking
Of fair Cresseid, sumtyme his awin darling.

Na wonder was, suppois in mynd that he
Tuik hir figure sa sone – and lo, now quhy:
The idole of ane thing in cace may be
Sa deip imprentit in the fantasy
That it deludis the wittis outwardly,
And sa appeiris in forme and lyke estait
Within the mynd as it was figurait.

Ane spark of lufe than till his hart culd spring
And kendlit all his bodie in ane fyre:
With hait fewir, ane sweit and trimbling
Him tuik, quhill he was reddie to expyre;
To beir his scheild his breist began to tyre;
Within ane quhyle he changit mony hew,
And nevertheles not ane ane uther knew.

For knichtlie pietie and memoriall
Of fair Cresseid, ane gyrdill can he tak,
Ane purs of gold, and mony gay jowall,
And in the skirt of Cresseid doun can swak;
Than raid away and not ane word he spak,
Pensive in hart, quhill he come to the toun,
And for greit cair oftsyis almaist fell doun.

Upon him then she cast up both her eyes
And at a glance it came into his thought
That he some time before had seen her face.
But she was in such state he knew her not;
Yet still into his mind her look had brought
The features and the amorous sweet glancing
Of fair Cresseid, one time his own, his darling.

No wonder then if in his mind he promptly
Received the likeness of her – this is why:
The image of a thing by chance may be
So deeply printed in the memory
That it deludes what's in the outer eye,
Presenting a form similar and twinned
To that which had been shaped within the mind.

A spark of love then sprang into his heart
And kindled his whole body in a fire.
A fever fit, hot tremblings and a sweat
Came over him: he was ready to expire.
The shield upon his shoulder made him tire.
Quickly and often his countenance changed hue
But neither, even so, the other knew.

For knightly piety and in remembrance
Of fair Cresseid, a girdle he took out,
A purse of gold and many shining gemstones,
And threw them down into Cresseid's skirt,
Then rode away and didn't speak a word,
Pensive in heart, until he reached the town
And often for great grief almost fell down.

The lipper folk to Cresseid than can draw
To se the equall distributioun
Of the almous, bot quhen the gold thay saw,
Ilkane to uther prevelie can roun,
And said; 'Yone lord hes mair affectioun,
However it be, unto yone lazarous
Than to us all; we knaw be his almous.'

'Quhat lord is yone,' quod scho, 'have ye na feill,
Hes done to us so greit humanitie?'
'Yes,' quod a lipper man, 'I knaw him weill;
Schir Troylus it is, gentill and fre.'
Quhen Cresseid understude that it was he,
Stiffer than steill thair stert ane bitter stound
Throwout hir hart, and fell doun to the ground.

Quhen scho ovircome, with siching sair and sad,
With mony cairfull cry and cald ochane:
'Now is my breist with stormie stoundis stad,
Wrappit in wo, ane wretch full will of wane!'
Than swounit scho oft or scho culd refrane,
And ever in hir swouning cryit scho thus;
'O fals Cresseid and trew knicht Troylus!

'Thy lufe, thy lawtie, and thy gentilnes
I countit small in my prosperitie,
Sa elevait I was in wantones,
And clam upon the fickill quheill sa hie.
All faith and lufe I promissit to the
Was in the self fickill and frivolous:
O fals Cresseid and trew knicht Troilus!

The lepers, to make sure the alms were doled
Equally among them, pressed together
Around Cresseid, but when they saw the gold
Each in secret whispered to the other,
'Yon lord has more affection for this leper
Than for the rest of us, whatever be
The sense of it. Look at this charity.'

'Yon lord,' she said, 'who is he, can you tell,
Who has shown us such great charity?'
'Yes,' said a leper man, 'I know him well,
Sir Troilus it is, high-born and free.'
When Cresseid understood that it was he,
A stun of pain, a stroke sharper than steel,
Went through her heart and to the ground she fell.

When she came to, she sighed sore and bewailed
Her woeful plight, and cried in desolation
'Now is my heart with gusts of grief assailed,
Swaddled in sadness, wretched and undone.'
Often she fainted before she quietened,
And in her fainting fits kept crying thus:
'O false Cresseid and true knight Troilus!

Your love, your loyalty, your noble ways
I took small notice of when I was happy,
Giddy and loose in loving as I was
And fixed upon the fickle wheel so high.
The love I vowed, the faith I plighted you
Were fickle in themselves and frivolous:
O false Cresseid and true knight Troilus!

'For lufe of me thow keipt gude continence,
Honest and chaist in conversatioun;
Of all wemen protectour and defence
Thou was, and helpit thair opinioun;
My mynd in fleschelie foull affectioun
Was inclynit to lustis lecherous:
Fy, fals Cresseid! O trew knicht Troylus!

'Lovers be war and tak gude heid about
Quhome that ye lufe, for quhome ye suffer paine.
I lat yow wit, thair is richt few thairout
Quhome ye may traist to have trew lufe agane;
Preif quhen ye will, your labour is in vaine.
Thairfoir I reid ye tak thame as ye find,
For thay ar sad as widdercok in wind.

'Becaus I knaw the greit unstabilnes,
Brukkill as glas, into my self, I say,
Traisting in uther als greit unfaithfulnes,
Als unconstant, and als untrew of fay –
Thocht sum be trew, I wait richt few ar thay;
Quha findis treuth, lat him his lady ruse!
Nane but myself as now I will accuse.'

Quhen this was said, with paper scho sat doun,
And on this maneir maid hir testament:
'Heir I beteiche my corps and carioun
With wormis and with taidis to be rent;
My cop and clapper, and myne ornament,
And all my gold the lipper folk sall have
Quhen I am deid, to burie me in grave.

For love of me you kept desire reined in,
Honourable and chaste in your behaviour.
Defender and protector of all women
You always were, their good names' guarantor.
But I with my hot flesh, my mind a fetor,
Was lustful, passionate and lecherous:
Fie, false Cresseid! O true knight Troilus!

Lovers beware and take good heed to whom
You give your love, for whom you suffer pain.
I tell you there are few enough among them
To be trusted to give true love back again.
Make proof, your effort will be proved in vain.
Therefore I urge you, take them as you find,
For their constancy's like weathercocks in wind.

Because I know in my own self how quick
I am to change, to snap like glass in two,
Because I assume that others are alike
Faithless, inconstant, light, I counsel you:
Though some be sound, I warrant they are few.
Who finds truth in his lady, let him praise her.
I myself will be my own accuser.'

When this was said, with paper she sat down
And made her testament as hereunder:
'I here commit my bodily remains
For earthworms and for toads to break and enter.
My cup and clapper, the ornaments I wore,
And all my gold the leper folk shall have
To pay for my interment and my grave.

'This royall ring set with this rubie reid,
Quhilk Troylus in drowrie to me send,
To him agane I leif it quhen I am deid,
To mak my cairfull deid unto him kend.
Thus I conclude schortlie, and mak ane end:
My spreit I leif to Diane, quhair scho dwellis,
To walk with hir in waist woddis and wellis.

'O Diomeid, thou hes baith broche and belt
Quhilk Troylus gave me in takning
Of his trew lufe!' and with that word scho swelt.
And sone ane lipper man tuik of the ring,
Syne buryt hir withouttin tarying;
To Troylus furthwith the ring he bair,
And of Cresseid the deith he can declair.

Quhen he had hard hir greit infirmitie,
Hir legacie and lamentatioun,
And how scho endit in sic povertie,
He swelt for wo and fell doun in ane swoun;
For greit sorrow his hart to brist was boun;
Siching full sadlie, said, 'I can no moir –
Scho was untrew and wo is me thairfoir.'

Sum said he maid ane tomb of merbell gray,
And wrait hir name and superscriptioun,
And laid it on hir grave quhair that scho lay,
In goldin letteris, conteining this ressoun:
'Lo, fair ladyis! Cresseid of Troyis toun,
Sumtyme countit the flour of womanheid,
Under this stane, lait lipper, lyis deid.'

This royal ring, set with this ruby red,
Which Troilus sent me for a love token,
I leave to him again when I am dead
To make my death and suffering known to him.
Thus I briefly end and make conclusion:
I leave my spirit to stray by paths and springs
With Diana in her wildwood wanderings.

O you have belt and brooch, both, Diomede,
That Troilus gave me for a sign and sealing
Of his true love,' and with those words she died.
Then soon a leper man took off the ring
And buried her. There was no tarrying.
Forthwith to Troilus the ring he carried
And made report of how Cresseid had died.

When he had listened to the whole story
Of her ordeal, her keen, her testament,
And how she ended in such poverty,
He swooned for grief and fell down in a faint.
The sorrow in his breast could scarce be pent.
Sighing hard, 'I can do', he said, 'no more.
She was untrue and woe is me therefore.'

Some said he made a tomb of marble grey
And wrote her name on it and an inscription
In golden letters, above where she lay
Inside her grave. These were the words set down:
'Lo, fair ladies, Cresseid of Troy town,
Accounted once the flower of womanhood,
Of late a leper, under this stone lies dead.'

Now, worthie wemen, in this ballet schort,
Maid for your worschip and instructioun,
Of cheritie, I monische and exhort,
Ming not your lufe with fals deceptioun.
Beir in your mynd this schort conclusioun
Of fair Cresseid, as I have said befoir.
Sen scho is deid, I speik of hir no moir.

Now, worthy women, in this short narration
Made in your honour and for your instruction,
For charity, I urge you and I caution:
Do not pollute your love with false deception.
Bear in mind the final quick declension
Of fair Cresseid, as I have told it here.
Since she is dead, I speak of her no more.

SEVEN FABLES

Thocht feinyeit fabils of ald poetré
Be not al grunded upon truth, yit than,
Thair polite termes of sweit rhetoré
Richt plesand ar unto the eir of man;
And als the cause that thay first began
Wes to repreif the haill misleving
Of man, be figure of ane uther thing.

In lyke maner as throw a bustious eird,
Swa it be laubourit with grit diligence,
Springis the flouris and the corne abreird,
Hailsum and gude to mannis sustenence;
Sa dois spring ane morall sweit sentence
Oute of the subtell dyte of poetry,
To gude purpois, quha culd it weill apply.

The nuttis schell, thocht it be hard and teuch,
Haldis the kirnell, and is delectabill;
Sa lyis thair ane doctrine wyse aneuch
And full of frute, under ane fenyeit fabill;
And clerkis sayis, it is richt profitabill
Amangis ernist to ming ane merie sport,
To light the spreit and gar the tyme be schort.

The Prologue

THE FABLES told by poets in old times
Are by no means all grounded upon truth
Yet their attractive style, their craft and themes
Still make for pleasant listening; and with
Good cause, since they, from the beginning,
Aimed to reprove man's whole wrong way of living
Under the figure of another thing.

Just as through a hard unyielding ground,
If it is laboured with real diligence,
The flowers will spring and young shoots of green corn,
Wholesome and good for human sustenance,
So sweetly edifying moral lessons
Spring from the well-worked plot of poetry
For those who have ears to hear and eyes to see.

The shell upon the nut, though hard and tough,
Holds the kernel and is still delightful.
Just so there lies a doctrine of great worth
And fruitfulness beneath a made-up fable.
And scholars say it is most profitable
To mix the merry in with graver matter:
It makes the spirit lift and time go quicker.

Forthermair, ane bow that ay is bent
Worthis unsmart and dullis on the string;
Sa dois the mynd that is ay diligent
In ernistfull thochtis and in studying.
With sad materis sum merines to ming
Accordis weill; thus Esope said, iwis,
Dulcius arrident seria picta iocis.

Of this authour, my maisteris, with your leif,
Submitting me to your correctioun,
In mother toung, of Latyng, I wald preif
To mak ane maner of translatioun –
Nocht of myself, for vane presumptioun,
Bot be requeist and precept of ane lord,
Of quhome the name it neidis not record.

In hamelie language and in termes rude
Me neidis wryte, forquhy of eloquence
Nor rethorike, I never understude.
Thairfoir meiklie I pray your reverence,
Gif ye find ocht that throw my negligence
Be deminute, or yit superfluous,
Correct it at your willis gratious.

My author in his fabillis tellis how
That brutal beistis spak and understude,
Into gude purpois dispute and argow,
Ane sillogisme propone, and eik conclude;
Putting exempill and similitude
How mony men in operatioun
Ar like to beistis in conditioun.

Furthermore, a bow that's always bent
Goes weak and gives and loses all its spring.
The same is true of minds always intent
On earnest thought and constant studying.
To alleviate what's sad by adding something
Cheerful is good; Aesop expressed it thus:
Dulcius arrident seria picta iocis.

Which author's Latin, masters, by your leave,
Submitting myself here to your correction,
I would convert to mother tongue and prove
Equal to the task of a translation –
Not out of vain presumption of my own,
But at the invitation of a lord
Whose name it is not needful to record.

In homely language and rough turns of speech
I have to write, for always eloquence
And rhetoric remained beyond my reach.
Therefore I humbly pray your reverence
That if you find here through my negligence
Anything much shortened – or protracted –
By your good will and good grace you'll correct it.

My author in his fables records how
Wild animals spoke sense and understood,
Debated point for point, could argue too,
Propound a syllogism and conclude;
He shows by example and similitude
How often humans in their own behaviour
Resemble the wild animals in nature.

Na mervell is, ane man be lyke ane beist,
Quhilk lufis ay carnall and foull delyte,
That schame can not him renye nor arreist,
Bot takis all the lust and appetyte,
Quhilk throw custum and the daylie ryte
Syne in the mynd sa fast is radicate
That he in brutal beist is transformate.

This nobill clerk, Esope, as I haif tauld,
In gay metir, facound and purperat,
Be figure wrait his buke, for he nocht wald
Tak the disdane off hie nor low estate;
And to begin, first of ane cok he wrate,
Seikand his meit, quhilk fand ane jolie stone,
Of quhome the fabill ye sall heir anone.

No wonder that a man grows like a beast!
Loving each carnal and each foul delight
Until no shame can hold or halt his lust,
He soon indulges every appetite
Which through repetition and bad habit
Roots in the mind so ineradicably
He is transformed: then bestiality.

This scholar, Aesop, as I have been telling,
Composed in verse of elegance and weight
A coded book, for he was unwilling
That readers high or low should underrate
His art; and first of a cock he wrote,
Hunting for food, that found a brilliant stone.
His is the fable you shall hear anon.

ANE COK SUM TYME with feddram fresch and gay,
Richt cant and crous, albeit he was bot pure,
Fleu furth upon ane dunghill sone be day;
To get his dennar set was al his cure.
Scraipand amang the as, be aventure
He fand ane jolie jasp, richt precious,
Wes castin furth in sweping of the hous.

As damisellis wantoun and insolent
That fane wald play and on the streit be sene,
To swoping of the hous thay tak na tent
Quhat be thairin, swa that the flure be clene;
Jowellis ar tint, as oftymis hes bene sene,
Upon the flure, and swopit furth anone.
Peradventure, sa wes the samin stone.

Sa mervelland upon the stane, quod he,
'O gentill Jasp, O riche and nobill thing,
Thocht I the find, thow ganis not for me;
Thow art ane jouell for ane lord or king.
Pietie it wer thow suld ly in this mydding,
Be buryit thus amang this muke and mold,
And thow so fair and worth sa mekill gold.

The Cock and the Jasper

A COCK ONE TIME, with feathers pert and bright,
Canty and bold, although he was dirt poor,
Rose and flew to a dunghill at first light,
An early bird, already to the fore,
Scraping away, when next thing in the stour
He finds this gemstone under dust and ashes,
Swept out by chance with sweepings from the house.

Giddy young ones, with their minds on nothing
But swanking in the street and being seen
Have little interest in their besoming.
They birl the brush to make the floor look clean.
So precious items dropped are very often
Swept from the doorstep out into the yard.
Something like that, in this case, had occurred.

He marvels at the stone and then says he,
'O jewel rare, O rich and noble thing,
I may have found you, but you're not for me.
You are a gemstone for a lord or king.
For you to be interred here in the dung
Is a great pity, down in the muck and mould,
And you so lovely and worth so much gold.

'It is pietie I suld the find, forquhy
Thy grit vertew, nor yit thy cullour cleir,
I may nouther extoll nor magnify,
And thow to me may mak bot lyttill cheir;
To grit lordis thocht thow be leif and deir,
I lufe fer better thing of les availl,
As draf or corne to fill my tume intraill.

'I had lever ga skraip heir with my naillis
Amangis this mow, and luke my lifys fude,
As draf or corne, small wormis, or snaillis,
Or ony meit wald do my stomok gude,
Than of jaspis ane mekill multitude;
And thow agane, upon the samin wyis
For les availl may me as now dispyis.

'Thow hes na corne, and thairof haif I neid;
Thy cullour dois bot confort to the sicht,
And that is not aneuch my wame to feid,
For wyfis sayis lukand werkis ar licht.
I wald sum meit have, get it geve I micht,
For houngrie men may not weill leve on lukis:
Had I dry breid, I compt not for na cukis.

'Quhar suld thow mak thy habitatioun?
Quhar suld thow duell, bot in ane royall tour?
Quhar suld thow sit, bot on ane kingis croun,
Exaltit in worschip and in grit honour?
Rise, gentill Jasp, of all stanis the flour,
Out of this fen, and pas quhar thow suld be:
Thow ganis not for me, nor I for the.'

'And a pity I should find you, who could never
Make clear hues like yours more sheer and clear
Nor prove your great worth any worthier:
Little about you gives me heart or cheer.
Let great lords cherish you and hold you dear.
Lesser things are better fit to tempt me,
Like corn or hogwash when my gizzard's empty.

'I'd rather be here scraping with my nails
In dust and dirt for dear life, hunting food –
The dregs and dross and little worms and snails
Or any grub at all that does me good –
I'd rather them than gems by the cartload.
While you, for your part, are uninterested
In anything that I desire or need.

'You don't have corn, and corn is what I covet.
Your colour calms the eye and feeds the sight
But colour's never going to feed my gullet.
I'm foraging from morning until night
And on the lookout always. But that's it!
How can I live on looks? It's food I need,
Not cooked or even hot: I'd eat dry bread.

'But where, gemstone, should be your habitation?
Where should you dwell but in a royal tower?
Where should you sit but on a royal crown
Exalted and installed in honour there?
Arise, Sir Jasper, fairest of the fair,
Shake off this filth and go where you should be.
I was not meant for you, nor you for me.'

Levand this jowell law upon the ground,
To seik his meit this cok his wayis went.
Bot quhen, or how, or quhome be it wes found,
As now I set to hald na argument.
Bot of the inward sentence and intent
Of this fabill, as myne author dois write,
I sall reheirs in rude and hamelie dite.

MORALITAS

This jolie jasp had properteis sevin:
The first, of cullour it was mervelous,
Part lyke the fyre and part lyke to the hevin;
It makis ane man stark and victorious,
Preservis als fra cacis perrillous;
Quha hes this stane sall have gude hap to speid,
Of fyre nor fallis him neidis not to dreid.

This gentill jasp, richt different of hew,
Betakinnis perfite prudence and cunning,
Ornate with mony deidis of vertew,
Mair excellent than ony eirthly thing,
Quhilk makis men in honour ay to ring,
Happie, and stark to wyn the victorie
Of all vicis and spirituall enemie.

Quha may be hardie, riche, and gratious?
Quha can eschew perrell and aventure?
Quha can governe ane realme, cietie, or hous
Without science? No man, I yow assure.
It is riches that ever sall indure,
Quhilk maith, nor moist, nor uther rust can freit:
To mannis saull it is eternall meit.

Leaving the jewel lying on the ground,
This cock went foraging upon his way.
But when or how or by whom it was found
I have no sure report, so cannot say.
But the inner point and import and idea
Behind the fable in the original
I shall rehearse in plain and homely style.

MORALITAS

The properties of this fair gem are seven:
First, as to colour, it is is marvellous,
Like fire partly, partly like the heaven.
It makes a man strong and victorious,
Preserves him too when things turn dangerous.
Whoever has this stone, good luck will favour:
No need for him to fear the fire or water.

This noble jasper, with its changing hue,
Signifies true wisdom and true learning
Perfected by the exercise of virtue
And far excelling any earthly thing.
This is what inclines men to good living
And makes them glad to strive, and fit to conquer
Every vice and spiritual danger.

Who's to be wealthy, kind, courageous?
Who is immune to chance and misadventure?
Who can take charge in home, town-hall or palace
And be a know-nothing? No one, for sure.
Knowledge is the wealth that will endure,
That rain won't ruin, nor moth nor rust devour.
To man's soul it is sustenance forever.

This cok, desyrand mair the sempill corne
Than ony jasp, may till ane fule be peir,
Quhilk at science makis bot ane moik and scorne,
And na gude can; als lytill will he leir –
His hart wammillis wyse argumentis to heir,
As dois ane sow to quhome men for the nanis
In hir draf-troich wald saw the precious stanis.

Quha is enemie to science and cunning
Bot ignorants, that understandis nocht
Quhilk is sa nobill, sa precious, and sa ding,
That it may not with eirdlie thing be bocht?
Weill wer that man, over all uther, that mocht
All his lyfe-dayis in perfite studie wair
To get science, for him neidis na mair.

Bot now, allace, this jasp is tynt and hid.
We seik it nocht, nor preis it for to find;
Haif we richis, na better lyfe we bid,
Of science thocht the saull be bair and blind.
Of this mater to speik, it wer bot wind,
Thairfore I ceis and will na forther say.
Ga seik the jasp, quha will, for thair it lay.

This cock, so obsessed with ordinary corn
He scorned a jasper, may in his ignorance
Be likened to a fool, who will scoff and scorn
At learning; impervious, thick, a dunce,
He takes a scunner at wise arguments,
The same as a sow that snotters in her gruel,
And spurns pearls in the trough, preferring swill.

Ignoramuses are the enemy
Of knowledge and of learning, and possess
No understanding of a thing so worthy,
So noble it is past all earthly price.
The luckiest man is one who spends his days
In study of the knowledge of the good:
A man like that fulfils his every need.

But now, alas, this jewel is lost and hid;
No one looks for it, no one pursues
The study of it. We make our wealth our god
And turn our souls to paupers, gain to lose.
But talk of this is like the wind that blows.
Therefore I conclude. I have said my say.
Look for the jewel who will, for there it lay.

Esope, MYNE AUTHOUR, *makis mentioun*
Of twa myis, and thay wer sisteris deir,
Of quham the eldest duelt in ane borous toun;
The uther wynnit uponland weill neir,
Soliter, quhyle under busk, quhyle under breir,
Quhilis in the corne, in uther mennis skaith,
As owtlawis dois, and levit on hir waith.

This rurall mous into the wynter tyde
Had hunger, cauld, and tholit grit distres;
The uther mous, that in the burgh can byde,
Was gild brother and made ane fre burges,
Toll-fre als, but custum mair or les,
And fredome had to ga quhairever scho list
Amang the cheis in ark, and meill in kist.

Ane tyme quhen scho wes full and unfutesair,
Scho tuke in mynd hir sister uponland,
And langit sair to heir of hir weilfair,
To se quhat lyfe scho led under the wand.
Bairfute, allone, with pykestaf in hir hand,
As pure pylgryme scho passit owt off town
To seik hir sister, baith oure daill and down.

The Two Mice

AESOP TELLS A TALE – Aesop, my author –
Of two mice who were sisters fair and fond.
The elder had a town-house in a borough.
The younger dwelt up country, near at hand
And by herself, at times on whinny ground,
At times in corn crops, living hand to mouth
Beyond the pale and off the land, by stealth.

This country mouse, when winter came, endured
Cold and hunger and extreme distress.
The other mouse, in town, sat on a board
With guild members, an independent burgess,
Exempt from tax, from port and market cess,
Free to go roaming wherever she liked best
Among the cheese and meal, in bin and chest.

One time, well-fed and lightsome on her feet,
She thought about her sister on the land
And wondered how she fared, what kind of state
She lived in, in the greenwood out beyond.
So, barefoot and alone, with staff in hand,
Like a poor pilgrim she set out from the town
To seek her sister, over dale and down.

Furth mony wilsum wayis can scho walk,
Throw mosse and mure, throw bankis, busk, and breir,
Fra fur to fur, cryand fra balk to balk,
'Cum furth to me, my awin sister deir!
Cry peip anis!' With that the mous culd heir
And knew hir voce, as kinnisman will do
Be verray kynd, and furth scho come hir to.

The hartlie joy, Lord God, geve ye had sene
Beis kithit quhen that thir sisteris met,
And grit kyndnes wes schawin thame betuene,
For quhylis thay leuch, and quhylis for joy thay gret,
Quhyle kissit sweit, quhylis in armis plet;
Ane thus thay fure quhill soberit wes their mude;
Syne fute for fute unto the chalmer yude.

As I hard say, it was ane sober wane,
Off fog and farne full misterlyk wes maid,
Ane sillie scheill under ane erdfast stane,
Off quhilk the entres wes not hie nor braid;
And in the samin thay went, but mair abaid,
Withoutin fyre or candill birnand bricht,
For comonly sic pykeris luffis not lycht.

Quhen thay wer lugit thus, thir sely myse,
The youngest sister into hir butterie hyid,
And brocht furth nuttis and peis, insteid off spyce;
Giff this wes gude fair, I do it on thame besyde.
This burges mous prompit forth in pryde,
And said, 'Sister, is this your dayly fude?'
'Quhy not,' quod scho, 'is not this meit richt gude?'

Through many wild and lonesome ways she goes,
By moss and moor, by bank and bush and briar,
Calling across the fallow land and furrows,
'Come out to me, my own sweet sister dear!
Just give one cheep.' With that the mouse could hear
And knew the voice, since it's in our nature
To recognise our own, and came to meet her.

If you had seen, Lord God! the high excitement
That overcame those sisters when they met,
The way the sighs passed back and forth between them,
The way they laughed and then for gladness wept!
They sweetly kissed, they held each other tight
And kept this up until they both grew calm,
Then went indoors together, arm in arm.

It was, as I have heard, a simple hut
Made expertly of foggage and of fern,
On stone supports sunk into earth upright,
The jambs set close, the lintel near the ground,
And into it they went and there remained.
No fire burned for them nor candle bright
For shady rooms best suit the fly-by-night.

When they were lodged and settled, these poor mice,
The younger sister to the pantry hurries
And brings out nuts and peas instead of spice.
Without being there, who'll say how good it was?
The burgess then gets haughty and pretentious,
And asks her sister, 'Is this how you eat?'
'Why,' she replies, 'is there something wrong with it?'

'Na, be my saull, I think it bot ane scorne.'
'Madame,' quod scho, 'ye be the mair to blame.
My mother sayd, sister, quhen we wer borne,
That I and ye lay baith within ane wame;
I keip the rate and custome off my dame,
And off my syre, levand in povertie,
For landis have we nane in propertie.'

'My fair sister,' quod scho, 'have me excusit –
This rude dyat and I can not accord.
To tender meit my stomok is ay usit,
Forquhy I fair als weill as ony lord.
Thir wydderit peis and nuttis, or thay be bord,
Will brek my teith and mak my wame full sklender,
Quhilk usit wes before to meitis tender.'

'Weil, weil, sister,' quod the rurall mous,
'Geve it pleis yow, sic thing as ye se heir,
Baith meit and dreink, harberie and hous,
Sal be your awin, will ye remane al yeir.
Ye sall it have wyth blyith and hartlie cheir,
And that suld mak the maissis that ar rude,
Amang freindis, richt tender, and wonder gude.

'Quhat plesure is in the feistis delicate,
The quhilkis ar gevin with ane glowmand brow?
Ane gentill hart is better recreate
With blyith visage, than seith to him ane kow.
Ane modicum is mair for till allow,
Swa that gude will be kerver at the dais,
Than thrawin vult and mony spycit mais.'

'No, by my soul, it's just so ordinary!'
'Madam,' she said, 'you are the more to blame.
When we were born I heard my mother say
The womb we both came out of was the same.
I'm true to her example and good name
And to my father's, to their frugal ways.
We own no lands or grounds or properties.'

'Please,' the reply came, 'let me be excused.
My tastes and this rough diet are at odds.
I live a lady's life now and am used
To tender meat; it's what my system needs.
These withered peas and nuts and shells and pods
Will break my teeth and hurt me in the stomach,
Now that I know what standards to expect.'

'Well, well, my sister,' says the country mouse,
'If you would like, and seeing that you're here,
You're welcome to the free run of the house
And food and drink. Stay on for the year!
It'll warm my heart to keep you and to share.
Our friendship matters more than middling food.
Who sniffs at cooking when the company's good?

'Delicacies pall, and fancy dishes,
When they are served up by a scowling face.
A sweetness in the giver's more delicious.
Fine sauces don't make up for lack of grace.
A modicum suffices, we do with less
When the carver carves from the goodness of his heart.
A sour-faced host can blink the best cook's art.'

For all hir mery exhortatioun,
This burges mous had littill will to sing,
Bot hevilie scho kest hir browis doun
For all the daynteis that scho culd hir bring;
Yit at the last scho said, halff in hething,
'Sister, this victuall and your royall feist
May weill suffice unto ane rurall beist.

'Lat be this hole and cum into my place:
I sall to yow schaw, be experience,
My Gude Friday is better nor your Pace,
My dische likingis is worth your haill expence.
I have housis anew off grit defence;
Off cat nor fall-trap I have na dreid.'
'I grant,' quod scho, and on togidder thay yeid.

In skugry ay, throw rankest gers and corne,
And under cowert prevelie couth thay creip;
The eldest wes the gyde and went beforne,
The younger to hir wayis tuke gude keip.
On nicht thay ran and on the day can sleip,
Quhill in the morning, or the laverok sang,
Thay fand the town, and in blythlie couth gang.

Not fer fra thyne unto ane worthie wane,
This burges brocht thame sone quhare thay suld be.
Withowt 'God speid' thair herberie wes tane
Into ane spence with vittell grit plentie:
Baith cheis and butter upon thair skelfis hie,
And flesche and fische aneuch, baith fresche and salt,
And sekkis full off grotis, meill, and malt.

In spite of all this well-disposed advice
The burgess was in no mood to be humoured.
She knit her brows above two glowering eyes,
No matter what choice pickings she was offered
Until, at last, she half-sighed and half-sneered,
'Sister, for a country mouse, this stuff
You've laid on makes a spread and is good enough.

'Give over this place, be my visitor
Come where I live, and learn when you're my guest
How my Good Friday's better than your Easter.
My dish-lickings more luscious than your feast.
My quarters are among the very safest.
Of cat or trap or trip I have no dread.'
'All right,' says sister, and they take the road.

Under cover, through clumps of corn and weed,
Keeping themselves hidden, on they creep.
The elder acts as guide and stays ahead.
The younger follows close and minds her step.
By night they make a run, by day they sleep,
Until one morning, when the lark was singing,
They reached the town and thankfully went in.

With none to greet or give them time of day,
The town mouse led on and they made their entry
To a residence not far along the way.
Next thing they stood inside a well-stocked pantry
With cheese and butter stacked on shelves, great plenty
Of red meat and hung game, fish fresh and salt,
Sacks full of groats, milled corn and meal and malt.

Efter, quhen thay disposit wer to dyne,
Withowtin grace, thay wesche and went to meit,
With all coursis that cukis culd devyne,
Muttoun and beif, strikin in tailyeis greit.
Ane lordis fair thus couth thay counterfeit
Except ane thing: thay drank the watter cleir
Insteid off wyne; bot yit thay maid gude cheir.

With blyith upcast and merie countenance,
The eldest sister sperit at hir gest
Giff that scho be ressone fand difference
Betuix that chalmer and hir sarie nest.
'Ye, dame,' quod scho, 'how lang will this lest?'
'For evermair, I wait, and langer to.'
'Giff it be swa, ye ar at eis,' quod scho.

Till eik thair cheir ane subcharge furth scho brocht –
Ane plait off grottis, and ane disch full off meill;
Thraf-caikkis als I trow scho spairit nocht
Aboundantlie about hir for to deill,
And mane full fyne scho brocht insteid off geill,
And ane quhyte candill owt off ane coffer stall
Insteid off spyce, to gust thair mouth withall.

This maid thay merie, quhill thay micht na mair,
And 'Haill, Yule, haill!' cryit upon hie.
Yit efter joy oftymes cummis cair,
And troubill efter grit prosperitie.
Thus as thay sat in all thair jolitie,
The spenser come with keyis in his hand,
Oppinnit the dure, and thame at denner fand.

Later, when they felt the urge to dine,
They washed their hands and sat, but said no grace.
There was every course a cook's art could design,
Roast beef and mutton relished slice by slice,
A meal fit for a lord. But they were mice
And showed it when they drank not wine but water,
Yet could hardly have enjoyed their banquet better.

Taunting and cajoling all at once,
The elder mouse enquired of her guest
Whether she thought there was real difference
Between that chamber and her sorry nest.
'Yes, ma'am,' said she, 'but how long will this last?'
'Forever, I expect, and even longer.'
'In that case, it's a safe house,' said the younger.

The town mouse, for their pleasure, produced more:
Groats on a plate and meal piled in a pan,
And didn't stay her hand, you can be sure,
When she doled the oatcakes out and served a scone
Of best white baker's bread instead of brawn,
Then stole a tall white candle from a chest
As a final touch, to give the meal more taste.

And so they revelled on and raised a cry,
And shouted 'Hail, Yule, hail!' and made merry.
Yet often care comes on the heels of joy
And trouble after great prosperity.
Thus, as they sat in all their jollity,
The steward comes along swinging his keys,
Opens the door and finds them at their ease.

Thay taryit not to wesche, as I suppose,
Bot on to ga, quha micht formest win.
The burges had ane hole, and in scho gois;
Hir sister had na hole to hyde hir in.
To se that selie mous, it wes grit sin;
So desolate and will off ane gude reid;
For verray dreid scho fell in swoun neir deid.

Bot, as God wald, it fell ane happie cace:
The spenser had na laser for to byde,
Nowther to seik nor serche, to sker nor chace,
Bot on he went, and left the dure up wyde.
The bald burges his passage weill hes spyde;
Out off hir hole scho come and cryit on hie,
'How fair ye, sister? Cry peip, quhairever ye be!'

This rurall mous lay flatling on the ground,
And for the deith scho wes full sair dredand,
For till hir hart straik mony wofull stound;
As in ane fever scho trimbillit, fute and hand.
And quhan hir sister in sic ply hir fand,
For verray pietie scho began to greit,
Syne confort hir with wordis hunny-sweit.

'Quhy ly ye thus? Ryse up, my sister deir!
Cum to your meit; this perrell is overpast.'
The uther answerit with hevie cheir,
'I may not eit, sa sair I am agast!
I had lever thir fourty dayis fast
With watter-caill, and to gnaw benis or peis,
Than all your feist in this dreid and diseis.'

They didn't wait to wash, as I imagine,
But rushed and raced and sped off desperately;
The burgess had a hole and in she went,
Her sister no such place of sanctuary.
To see that mouse in panic was great pity,
In dread, bewildered, cornered and astray
So that she swooned and nearly passed away.

But God had willed and worked a happy outcome:
The hard-pressed steward could not afford to bide.
He hadn't time to harry or to hunt them
But hurried on, and left the room-door wide.
The burgess watched him make his way outside,
Then scooted from her hole and cried on high,
'How are you, sister? Where? Just cheep for me!'

Sure she was doomed, and terrified to die,
This country mouse lay on the ground prostrate.
Her heart beat fast, she was like somebody
Shaken by fever, trembling hand and foot,
And when her sister found her in this state
For very pity she broke down in tears,
Then spoke these words, sweet honey to her ears:

'Why do you cower like this, dear sister? Rise!
Return to table. Come. The danger's past.'
The other answered in a stricken voice,
'I cannot eat, I am so sore aghast.
I'd rather do Lent's forty days of fast
On cabbage water, gnawing peas and beans,
Than feast with you here in such dread conditions.'

With fair tretie yit scho gart hir upryse,
And to the burde thay went and togidder sat.
And scantlie had thay drunkin anis or twyse,
Quhen in come Gib Hunter, our jolie cat,
And bad 'God speid.' The burges up with that,
And till hir hole scho fled as fyre of flint;
Bawdronis the uther be the bak hes hint.

Fra fute to fute he kest hir to and fra,
Quhylis up, quhylis down, als cant as ony kid.
Quhylis wald he lat hir rin under the stra;
Quhylis wald he wink, and play with hir buk-heid;
Thus to the selie mous grit pane he did;
Quhill at the last throw fortune and gude hap,
Betwix ane dosor and the wall scho crap.

And up in haist behind the parraling
Scho clam so hie that Gilbert micht not get hir,
Syne be the cluke thair craftelie can hing
Till he wes gane; hir cheir wes all the better.
Syne doun scho lap quhen thair wes nane to let hir,
And to the burges mous loud can scho cry,
'Fairweill, sister, thy feist heir I defy!

'Thy mangerie is mingit all with cair;
Thy guse is gude, thy gansell sour as gall;
The subcharge off thy service is bot sair;
Sa sall thow find heir-efterwart ma fall.
I thank yone courtyne and yone perpall wall
Off my defence now fra yone crewell beist.
Almichtie God keip me fra sic ane feist.

Still, being soothed so sweetly, she got up
And went to table where again they sat,
But hardly had they time to drink one cup
When in comes Hunter Gib, our jolly cat,
And bids good day. The burgess ups with that
And speedy as the spark from flint makes off.
His nibs then takes the other by the scruff.

From foot to foot he chased her to and fro,
Whiles up, whiles down, as quick as any kid,
Whiles letting her go free beneath the straw,
Whiles playing blind man's buff with her, shut-eyed.
And thus he kept that poor mouse in great dread,
Until by lucky chance, at the last call,
She slipped between the hangings and the wall.

Then up in haste behind the tapestry
She climbed so high that Gilbert couldn't get her
And hung there by the claws most capably
Till he was gone; and when her mood was better
And she could move with no cat to upset her
Down she came on the town mouse, shouting out,
'Sister, farewell. Your feast I set at nought.

'Your spread is spoiled, your cream in curds from worry.
Your goose is good, your sauce as sour as gall,
Your second helpings sure to make you sorry,
Mishaps still sure to haunt you and befall.
I thank that curtain and partition-wall
For guarding me against yon cruel beast.
Save me, Almighty God, from such a feast.

'Wer I into the kith that I come fra,
For weill nor wo I suld never cum agane.'
With that scho tuke hir leif and furth can ga,
Quhylis throw the corne, and quhylis throw the plane.
Quhen scho wes furth and fre scho wes full fane,
And merilie markit unto the mure;
I can not tell how eftirwart scho fure,

Bot I hard say scho passit to hir den,
Als warme as woll, suppose it wes not greit,
Full beinly stuffit, baith but and ben,
Off beinis and nuttis, peis, ry, and quheit;
Quhenever scho list scho had aneuch to eit,
In quyet and eis withoutin ony dreid,
Bot to hir sisteris feist na mair scho yeid.

MORALITAS

Freindis, heir may ye find, and ye will tak heid,
Into this fabill ane gude moralitie:
As fitchis myngit ar with nobill seid,
Swa intermellit is adversitie
With eirdlie joy, swa that na estate is frie
Without trubill and sum vexatioun,
And namelie thay quhilk clymmis up maist hie,
That ar not content with small possessioun.

Blissed be sempill lyfe withoutin dreid;
Blissed be sober feist in quietie.
Quha hes aneuch, of na mair hes he neid,
Thocht it be littill into quantatie.
Grit aboundance and blind prosperitie
Oftymes makis ane evill conclusioun;

'If I were back on home ground, I would stay,
Never, for weal or woe, come forth again.'
With that she took her leave and went her way,
Now through the corn, now on the open plain,
Glad to be on the loose and given rein
To gambol and be giddy on the moor.
What then became of her I can't be sure,

Though I have heard she made it to her nest
That was as warm as wool, if small and strait,
Packed snugly from back wall to chimney breast
With peas and nuts and beans and rye and wheat.
When she inclined, she had enough to eat
In peace and quiet there, amidst her store,
But to her sister's house she went no more.

MORALITAS

Friends, you will find, if only you'll take heed,
This fable masks a good morality.
As vetches are mixed in with wholesome seed
So intermingled is adversity
With joy on earth, and no class is free
Of trouble or their share of tribulation,
But the discontented ones especially,
Climbers with a craving for possessions.

Blessed be simple life lived free of dread;
And blessed be a frugal decency.
Whoever has enough is not in need,
No matter how reduced his portion be.
Abundance, comfort, blind prosperity
Often prove the last and worst illusion:

The sweitest lyfe, thairfoir, in this cuntrie,
Is sickernes with small possessioun.

O wantoun man, that usis for to feid
Thy wambe, and makis it a god to be;
Luke to thyself, I warne the weill, but dreid.
The cat cummis, and to the mous hes ee;
Quhat vaillis than thy feist and royaltie,
With dreidfull hart and tribulatioun?
Best thing in eird, thairfor, I say for me,
Is blyithnes in hart, with small possessioun.

Thy awin fyre, freind, thocht it be bot ane gleid,
It warmis weill, and is worth gold to the;
And Solomon sayis, gif that thow will reid,
'Under the hevin I can not better be
Than ay be blyith and leif in honestie.'
Quhairfoir I may conclude be this ressoun:
Of eirthly joy it beiris maist degré,
Blyithnes in hart, with small possessioun.

So to be safe, not sorry in this country
Content yourself with just a few possessions.

O self-indulgent man, glutton for food,
Worshipper of your own pampered belly,
Be on your guard! Beware and take good heed:
Cat prowls and you're the mouse in that cat's eye.
Your feast and fashion are no guarantee
Of peace of mind, sweet thought in quiet sessions.
For happiness on earth, therefore, I say,
Content yourself with just a few possessions.

Friend, your own fireside, though flame be dead,
Is still the warmest and the place to be;
And Solomon's wise words you will have read,
'Under heaven there is no better way
To happiness than living virtuously.'
Wherefore I end with this reassertion:
To live on earth and know the greatest joy,
Content yourself with just a few possessions.

In middis of June, that sweit seasoun,
Quhen that fair Phebus with his bemis bricht
Had dryit up the dew fra daill and doun,
And all the land maid with his lemis licht,
In ane mornyng betuix mid day and nicht
I rais and put all sleuth and sleip asyde,
And to ane wod I went allone but gyde.

Sweit wes the smell off flouris quhyte and reid,
The noyes off birdis richt delitious,
The bewis braid blomit abone my heid,
The ground growand with gers gratious;
Off all plesance that place wes plenteous,
With sweit odouris and birdis harmony;
The morning myld – my mirth wes mair forthy.

The rosis reid arrayit on rone and ryce,
The prymeros and the purpour violat bla;
To heir it wes ane poynt off Paradice,
Sic mirth the mavis and the merle couth ma;
The blossummis blythe brak up on bank and bra;
The smell off herbis and off fowlis cry,
Contending quha suld have the victory.

The Lion and the Mouse

IT WAS IN THAT SWEET SEASON, middle June,
When Phoebus with his fair beams shining bright
Had dried the dew off every dale and down
And clad the land in raiment made of light:
One morning as the sun climbed to its height
I rose and cast all sloth and sleep aside
And wandered on my own out to a wood.

Sweet was the smell of flowers, white and red,
The singing of the birds a sheer delight.
Broad boughs were in full bloom above my head.
Rich herbs and herbage flourished at my feet.
All pleasure and all plenty seemed to meet
In fragrances and birdsong in that place.
And the mild morning made me more rejoice.

Red roses blossoming on twig and bush,
The primrose and the violet, purplish-blue:
The jubilating blackbird and the thrush
Were paradise on earth to listen to.
The banks and braes in bloom made a fine show.
And scented herbs and the small birds crying –
All these things in contention, sweetly vying.

Me to conserve than fra the sonis heit,
Under the schaddow off ane hawthorne grene
I lenit doun amang the flouris sweit,
Syne cled my heid and closit baith my ene.
On sleip I fell amang thir bewis bene,
And in my dreme, me thocht come throw the schaw
The fairest man that ever befoir I saw.

His gowne wes off ane claith als quhyte as milk,
His chemeris wes off chambelate purpour broun,
His hude off scarlet, bordowrit weill with silk
On hekillit wyis untill his girdill doun,
His bonat round, and off the auld fassoun,
His beird wes quhyte, his ene wes grit and gray,
With lokker hair quhilk over his schulderis lay.

Ane roll off paper in his hand he bair,
Ane swannis pen stikand under his eir,
Ane inkhorne, with ane prettie gilt pennair,
Ane bag off silk, all at his belt can beir.
Thus wes he gudelie grathit in his geir,
Off stature large, and with ane feirfull face.
Evin quhair I lay he come ane sturdie pace,

And said, 'God speid, my sone', and I wes fane
Off that couth word, and off his cumpany.
With reverence I salusit him agane,
'Welcome, father', and he sat doun me by.
'Displeis yow not, my gude maister, thocht I
Demand your birth, your facultye, and name;
Quhy ye come heir, or quhair ye dwell at hame.'

To keep myself out of the burning sun,
I lay among sweet-smelling flowers, at ease
Beneath a hawthorn tree in shadows green,
Then covered up my head and closed my eyes.
I fell asleep beneath those balmy boughs
And dreamt I saw come towards me through the wood
The handsomest man I ever had encountered.

His gown was made of cloth as white as milk,
His outer cloak of camlet, murky purple,
His hood of scarlet, bordered well with silk
Hanging down like hackles to his girdle.
His bonnet round, in the old-fashioned style.
Beard white; eyes wide and grey; a head of hair
That curled and lay in locks upon each shoulder.

He carried in his hand a roll of paper.
A swan's-quill pen stuck out behind his ear.
An inkhorn, a neat gilt pen container
And silken pouch hung from the belt he wore.
Thus was he tackled trimly in his gear,
Of stature large, imposing countenance.
Then up to where I lay he made advance

Saying, 'God bless you, son', and I was glad
Of those warm words and of his company.
I greeted him respectfully and said,
'Welcome, father', and as he sat by me
Went on, 'My good master, may I kindly
Ask who you are, your profession and your name,
Why you come here, and where you call your home?'

'My sone,' said he, 'I am off gentill blude;
My native land is Rome, withoutin nay,
And in that towne first to the sculis I yude,
In civile law studyit full mony ane day,
And now my winning is in hevin for ay.
Esope I hecht; my writing and my werk
Is couth and kend to mony cunning clerk.'

'O maister Esope, poet lawriate,
God wait ye ar full deir welcum to me!
Ar ye not he that all thir fabillis wrate,
Quhilk in effect, suppois thay fenyeit be,
Ar full off prudence and moralitie?'
'Fair sone,' said he, 'I am the samin man.'
God wait gif that my hert wes merie than.

I said, 'Esope, my maister venerabill,
I yow beseik hartlie for cheritie,
Ye wald dedene to tell ane prettie fabill
Concludand with ane gude moralitie.'
Schaikand his heid, he said, 'My sone, lat be,
For quhat is it worth to tell ane fenyeit taill,
Quhen haly preiching may nathing availl?

'Now in this warld me think richt few or nane
To Goddis word that hes devotioun;
The eir is deif, the hart is hard as stane;
Now oppin sin without correctioun,
The hart inclynand to the eirth ay doun.
Sa roustit is the warld with canker blak
That now my taillis may lytill succour mak.'

'My son,' said he, 'I am a well-born man.
None will deny my native place is Rome –
And I got my early schooling in that town.
I studied civil law there a long time
And now forever heaven is my home.
My name is Aesop: works that I have written
Are known and conned by many a learned man.'

'O master Aesop, poet laureate,
God knows you are most welcome here to me
For are you not the very one who write
Those fables, which are make-believe, maybe,
But full of wisdom and morality?'
'Fair son,' said he, 'I am that selfsame man.'
God knows indeed my heart was happy then.

'Aesop,' I said, 'my master venerable,
Grant, I pray, this most heartfelt petition:
Deign to tell me, please, a well-turned fable
Leading to a good moral conclusion.'
He shook his head and answered, 'Ah, my son,
What good is it to tell a made-up tale
When holy preachers preach to no avail?

'In this world now, it seems that few or none
Hear the word of God with due devotion.
Their ears are deaf, their hearts as hard as stone.
Sin is blatant, flaunts without correction,
And earthbound instinct drags the pure heart down.
The world's so rotted, bletted, cankered black,
My tales are told to small or no effect.'

'Yit, gentill schir,' said I, *'for my requeist,*
Not to displeis your fatherheid, I pray,
Under the figure off ane brutall beist,
Ane morall fabill ye wald denye to say.
Quha wait nor I may leir and beir away
Sum thing thairby heirefter may availl?'
'I grant,' quod he, *and thus begouth ane taill:*

*

Ane lyoun, at his pray wery foirrun,
To recreat his limmis and to rest,
Beikand his breist and belly at the sun,
Under ane tre lay in the fair forest;
Swa come ane trip off myis out off thair nest,
Richt tait and trig, all dansand in ane gyis,
And over the lyoun lansit twyis or thryis.

He lay so still, the myis wes not effeird,
Bot to and fro out over him tuke thair trace;
Sum tirlit at the campis off his beird,
Sum spairit not to claw him on the face;
Merie and glaid, thus dansit thay ane space,
Till at the last the nobill lyoun woke,
And with his pow the maister mous he tuke.

Scho gave ane cry, and all the laif, agast,
Thair dansing left and hid thame sone alquhair.
Scho that wes tane cryit and weipit fast,
And said allace oftymes that scho come thair:
'Now am I tane ane wofull presonair,
And for my gilt traistis incontinent
Off lyfe and deith to thoill the jugement.'

'Yet, gentle sir,' said I, 'I would request –
Not to disrespect your reservation –
That you would frame a tale around a beast,
A fable with a moral, a narration
That might contribute to my education,
Something worth remembering.' 'Well, I shall,'
Said Aesop, and proceeded with this tale:

*

A hunting lion, tired from his run,
Needing to catch his breath and have a rest
Lay warming breast and belly in the sun
Under a tree in a pleasant forest.
Next thing a troop of mice skips from their nest,
Nifty and nimble, dancing briskly round,
And step-dance two or three times on the lion.

He lay so still the mice were not afraid,
But advanced, retired, jigged and reeled apace,
Some plucking at the whiskers of his beard,
Some bold enough to scratch him in the face,
Lightsome and blithe, the merriest of mice,
Till the noble lion woke at last and pounced
And clamped down on the one who led the dance.

She gave a cry, and the rest all cried, aghast,
And scattered and hid hurriedly wherever.
The leader in the lion's paw held fast
Laments 'Alas, alas', and weeps in terror.
'O woe me,' she wails, 'I'm a prisoner,
And must face trial now for my offence.
My life and death hang trembling in the balance.'

Than spak the lyoun to that cairfull mous:
'Thow cative wretche and vile unworthie thing,
Over-malapart and eik presumpteous
Thow wes, to mak out over me thy tripping.
Knew thow not weill I wes baith lord and king
Off beistis all?' 'Yes,' quod the mous, 'I knaw,
Bot I misknew, because ye lay so law.

'Lord, I beseik thy kinglie royaltie,
Heir quhat I say, and tak in patience.
Considder first my simple povertie,
And syne thy mychtie hie magnyfycence;
Se als how thingis done off neglygence,
Nouther off malice nor of presumptioun,
The rather suld have grace and remissioun.

'We wer repleit, and had grit aboundance
Off alkin thingis, sic as to us effeird;
The sweit sesoun provokit us to dance
And mak sic mirth as nature to us leird;
Yet lay so still and law upon the eird
That be my sawll we weind ye had bene deid –
Elles wald we not have dancit over your heid.'

'Thy fals excuse', the lyoun said agane,
'Sall not availl ane myte, I underta.
I put the cace, I had bene deid or slane,
And syne my skyn bene stoppit full off stra;
Thocht thow had found my figure lyand swa,
Because it bare the prent off my persoun,
Thow suld for feir on kneis have fallin doun.

The lion spoke then to that stricken mouse,
'You miserable, despicable, mean thing,
Overly familiar and presumptuous,
Treating my person as your dancing ring:
Do you not know I am both lord and king
Of all the beasts?' 'Yes,' said the mouse, 'I do,
But you lay so quiet there, I mistook you.

'So, my lord, I beseech your majesty
To hear my plea and attend in patience.
Take good account first of my poverty
And then consider your magnificence.
Consider too how simple negligence –
A thing not done with malice or presumption –
Should sooner receive gracious remission.

'We'd had our fill, enjoyed in great abundance
The proper dues and needs of our condition;
The pleasant season prompted us to dance
And sport ourselves in our own natural fashion.
You lay so still, had such a dead expression,
We thought, by my soul, that you were dead indeed.
Why else would we have danced upon your head?'

'This is a false excuse,' the lion said,
'And will not in the least, be warned, avail.
Supposing that I had indeed been dead
And what you'd found was a stuffed animal,
A straw lion, my skin alone, then still
You should have been in awe and kneeling down
Because it bore the imprint of my person.

'For thy trespas thow can mak na defence,
My nobill persoun thus to vilipend;
Off thy feiris, nor thy awin negligence,
For to excuse thow can na cause pretend;
Thairfoir thow suffer sall ane schamefull end
And deith, sic as to tressoun is decreit –
Onto the gallous harlit be the feit.'

'Na! mercie, lord, at thy gentrice I ase,
As thow art king off beistis coronate,
Sober thy wraith, and let thi yre overpas,
And mak thy mynd to mercy inclynate.
I grant offence is done to thyne estate,
Quhairfoir I worthie am to suffer deid,
Bot gif thy kinglie mercie reik remeid.

'In everie juge mercy and reuth suld be
As assessouris and collaterall;
Without mercie, justice is crueltie,
As said is in the lawis speciall:
Quhen rigour sittis in the tribunall,
The equitie off law quha may sustene?
Richt few or nane, but mercie gang betwene.

'Alswa ye knaw the honour triumphall
Off all victour upon the strenth dependis
Off his conqueist, quhilk manlie in battell
Throw jeopardie of weir lang defendis.
Quhat pryce or loving, quhen the battell endis,
Is said off him that overcummis ane man
Him to defend quhilk nouther may nor can?

'Your crime is such you have no defence.
What you've committed is *lèse-majesté*.
There is no case, you have no arguments
To absolve yourself or those accessory.
Wherefore your disgraceful doom shall be
To suffer death, as is decreed for treason –
And mount the gallows, struggling and squealing.'

'Ah no, my lord, I beseech your royal grace
As crowned head of the beasts to moderate
Your anger: let your fit of fury pass,
Let mercy change your mind, be temperate.
Your honour has been injured, I admit,
And I deserve the sentence you decree –
Unless you relent, my lord, and pardon me.

'In every judge, mercy and compassion
Should act as learned friends and counsellors.
Justice is cruelty when mercy's wanting
As the highest, holiest law we know allows.
When rigour won't relent and sits and glowers
Who will believe the bench impartial? None
Or very few, unless there is compassion.

'When it comes to martial honour too you know
The value of a victory depends
Upon the strength of the opponent, how
Fiercely he fights or manfully defends.
What praise or honour, when the battle ends,
Is due to one whose foe would not or could not
Stand to and meet and match him in the fight?

'Ane thowsand myis to kill and eik devoir
Is lytill manheid to ane strang lyoun;
Full lytill worschip have ye wyn thairfoir,
To qwhais strenth is na comparisoun.
It will degraid sum part off your renoun
To sla ane mous, quhilk may mak na defence
Bot askand mercie at your excellence.

'Also it semis not your celsitude,
Quhilk usis daylie meittis delitious,
To fyle your teith or lippis with my blude,
Quhilk to your stomok is contagious.
Unhailsum meit is of ane sarie mous,
And that namelie untill ane strang lyoun,
Wont till be fed with gentill vennesoun.

'My lyfe is lytill worth, my deith is les,
Yit and I leif, I may peradventure
Supplé your hienes beand in distres;
For oft is sene, ane man off small stature
Reskewit hes ane lord off hie honour,
Keipit that wes, in poynt to be overthrawin;
Throw misfortoun sic cace may be your awin.'

Quhen this wes said, the lyoun his language
Paissit, and thocht according to ressoun,
And gart mercie his cruell ire asswage,
And to the mous grantit remissioun,
Oppinnit his pow, and scho on kneis fell doun,
And baith hir handis unto the hevin upheild,
Cryand, 'Almichty God mot yow foryeild!'

'To kill and then devour a thousand mice –
What's manly about that in a great lion?
The weaker the defeated is, the less
Enhanced is a strong conqueror's renown.
It will demean and mar your reputation
To kill a mouse whose one defence was free
Reliance on your excellency's mercy.

'Moreover, it's below your majesty
Whose diet day by day is so delicious
To soil your teeth and lips by eating me.
My blood would turn your stomach and cause illness.
There is infection in the meat of mice
To which lions, in particular, are prone,
Used as they are to noble venison.

'My life's of little value, my death less.
Yet if I live, who knows, it could happen
I'd help your highness in a chance distress,
For often one who seems in no condition
To rescue some imperilled lord from prison
Will prove to be the only one who can.
Which case, if fortune failed, could be your own.'

When this was said, the lion reconsidered.
His anger was assuaged, he heeded reason,
And letting mercy moderate his hard
Pronouncement, granted the mouse remission,
Opened his paw and dropped her. She fell down,
Then reached her two hands heavenward and cried,
'Almighty God reward you for this deed.'

Quhen scho wes gone, the lyoun held to hunt,
For he had nocht, bot levit on his pray,
And slew baith tayme and wyld, as he wes wont,
And in the cuntrie maid ane grit deray;
Till at the last the pepill fand the way
This cruell lyoun how that thay mycht tak:
Off hempyn cordis strang nettis couth thay mak,

And in ane rod, quhair he wes wont to ryn,
With raipis rude fra tre to tre it band;
Syne kest ane range on raw the wod within,
With hornis blast and kennettis fast calland.
The lyoun fled, and throw the ron rynnand
Fell in the net and hankit fute and heid;
For all his strenth he couth mak na remeid,

Welterand about with hiddeous rummissing,
Quhyle to, quhyle fra, quhill he mycht succour get.
Bot all in vane – it vailyeit him nathing –
The mair he flang, the faster wes the net.
The raipis rude wes sa about him plet
On everilk syde that succour saw he nane,
Bot styll lyand and murnand maid his mane.

'O lamit lyoun, liggand heir sa law,
Quhair is the mycht off thy magnyfycence,
Off quhome all brutall beist in eird stude aw,
And dred to luke upon thy excellence?
But hoip or help, but succour or defence,
In bandis strang heir man I ly, allace,
Till I be slane; I se nane uther grace.

When she was gone, the lion went to hunt
Since he never gathered food but lived on prey,
Killing both wild and tame, as was his wont,
Spreading terror over the whole country
Until at last the people found a way
To trap this cruel lion. From hemp cord
They wove strong nets and set them in the road

The lion used when he was on the prowl,
Stretching them tight across from tree to tree;
Then lined up in the wood to await the kill.
The hounds and horns create a wild melee.
Along the road the lion starts to flee,
Trips on the net, gets tangled head and foot,
And for all his strength and struggle, can't get out.

He turned and twisted, gave a hideous roar,
Strained, contorted, kicked this way and that,
But all to no avail. His reign was over.
The more he turned, the tighter drew the net,
The purchase of the ropes being so complete
On every part of him; and thus forlorn,
He ceased his struggle and began to mourn.

'O crippled lion, lying here so low,
Where is the power of your magnificence
Of which earth's animals all stood in awe
And feared to look upon your countenance?
No hope or help, no succour or defence
Are left to me. Alas, I am tied down
In sturdy bonds and certain to be slain.

'Thair is na wy that will my harmis wreik
Nor creature do confort to my croun.
Quha sall me bute? Quha sall my bandis breik?
Quha sall me put fra pane off this presoun?'
Be he had maid this lamentatioun,
Throw aventure, the lytill mous come neir,
And off the lyoun hard the pietuous beir;

And suddanlie it come intill hir mynd
That it suld be the lyoun did hir grace,
And said, 'Now wer I fals and richt unkynd
Bot gif I quit sumpart thy gentrace
Thow did to me', and on this way scho gais
To hir fellowis, and on thame fast can cry,
'Cum help! cum help!' and thay come all in hy.

'Lo,' quod the mous, 'this is the samin lyoun
That grantit grace to me quhen I wes tane,
And now is fast heir bundin in presoun,
Brekand his hart with sair murning and mane;
Bot we him help, off souccour wait he nane.
Cum help to quyte ane gude turne for ane uther;
Go, lous him sone!' and thay said, 'Ye, gude brother.'

Thay tuke na knyfe – thair teith wes scharpe anewch;
To se that sicht, forsuith, it wes grit wounder –
How that they ran amang the rapis tewch,
Befoir, behind, sum yeid abone, sum under,
And schuir the raipis off the net in-schunder;
Syne bad him ryse, and he start up anone,
And thankit thame; syne on his way is gone.

'There's nobody to right my wrongs and wreak
Vengeance for me, none to respect my crown.
Who'll help me now? Come to my aid and break
These bonds, release me from this prison?'
The minute he had made this lamentation
It so happened the little mouse came by
And overheard the lion's grievous cry.

And suddenly it came into her mind
This was the lion who had pardoned her,
Saying, 'I'd be unnatural and unkind
Not to repay in some small part the favour
You graciously did me', and so she called her
Companions loud and long, repeatedly,
To come and help, which they did immediately.

'Look,' said the mouse, 'this is that same lion
Who pardoned me when I was in his power.
Now here he lies, heartbroken, making moan
Like a prisoner tied up inside a tower.
Unless we help, he cannot hope for succour.
But one good turn deserves another, so,
Do we free him?' 'Sister,' they said, 'we do.'

They took no knife, their teeth where sharp enough –
To watch them at their work was a great wonder:
It didn't matter that the ropes were tough,
They went for them, top, bottom, over, under,
Bit bindings till the net just fell asunder,
Then bade him rise. He sprang immediately
Up on his feet with thanks; and went his way.

Now is the lyoun fre off all danger,
Lows and delyverit to his libertie
Be lytill beistis off ane small power,
As ye have hard, because he had pietie.
Quod I, 'Maister, is thair ane moralitie
In this fabill?' 'Yea, sone,' he said, 'richt gude.'
'I pray yow, schir,' quod I, 'ye wald conclude.'

MORALITAS

As I suppois, this mychtie gay lyoun
May signifie ane prince or empriour,
Ane potestate, or yit ane king with croun –
Quhilk suld be walkrife gyde and governour
Of his pepill – that takis na labour
To reule and steir the land, and justice keip,
Bot lyis still in lustis, sleuth, and sleip.

The fair forest with levis, lowne and le,
With foulis sang and flouris ferlie sweit,
Is bot the warld and his prosperitie,
As fals plesance, myngit with cair repleit.
Richt as the rois with froist and wynter weit
Faidis, swa dois the warld, and thame desavis
Quhilk in thair lustis maist confidence havis.

Thir lytill myis ar bot the commountie,
Wantoun, unwyse, without correctioun;
Thair lordis and princis quhen that thay se
Of justice mak nane executioun,
Thay dreid nathing to mak rebellioun
And disobey, for quhy thay stand nane aw,
That garris thame thair soveranis misknaw.

The lion is at large now, out of danger,
Loosed and delivered, set at liberty
By little beasts, possessed of little power,
Because, as you have heard, he showed them pity
'Master,' I asked, 'does a morality
Attach to this fable?' 'Yes,' he said, 'a good one.'
'Please,' I said then, 'share it, in conclusion.'

MORALITAS

This mighty lion, to my way of thinking,
May signify a prince or emperor
Or any potentate – say a crowned king –
Who should be a sure guide and governor
Of his nation, rule and administer
Justice in the land, but whose control
Slips as dull sloth and lust possess his soul.

The pleasant sheltered forest, calm and leafy,
With its birdsong and delightful flowers
Stands for the world and its prosperity
Where sorrows stalk and shadow empty pleasures.
Just as the rose fades, faced with the cold winter's
Frost and wet, so does the world play false
To those flushed up with lustful self-indulgence.

These little mice are the common people,
Thoughtless, wilful, without discipline,
Who, seeing princes and their lords neglectful
Of justice and its proper execution
Have no fear of rising in rebellion
And disobeying, since the dread is gone
That kept them subject to their sovereign.

Be this fabill, ye lordis of prudence
May considder the vertew of pietie,
And to remit sumtyme ane grit offence,
And mitigate with mercy crueltie.
Oftymis is sene ane man of small degré
Hes quit ane kinbute, baith of gude and ill,
As lord hes done rigour or grace him till.

Quha wait how sone ane lord of grit renoun,
Rolland in wardlie lust and vane plesance,
May be overthrawin, destroyit, and put doun
Throw fals Fortoun, quhilk of all variance
Is haill maistres, and leidar of the dance
Till injust men, and blindis thame so soir
That thay na perrell can provyde befoir?

Thir rurall men, that stentit hes the net
In quhilk the lyoun suddandlie wes tane,
Waittit alway amendis for to get,
For hurt men wrytis in the marbill stane.
Mair till expound, as now, I lett allane,
Bot king and lord may weill wit quhat I mene:
Figure heirof oftymis hes bene sene.

Quhen this wes said, quod Esope, 'My fair child,
I the beseik and all men for to pray
That tressoun of this cuntrie be exyld,
And justice regne, and lordis keip thair fay
Unto thair soverane lord baith nycht and day.'
And with that word he vanist and I woke;
Syne throw the schaw my journey hamewart tuke.

By means of this fable then Your Worships
May take into consideration pity,
Learn sometimes to pardon great relapse
And mitigate your cruelty with mercy,
For it often chances a man of low degree
Will give back as he got according as
His lord to him was merciful or harsh.

Who knows how soon a lord of high renown,
But slovenly, degraded, carnal, vain,
Will suffer ruin and be overthrown
By Fortune, that false mistress and the main
Decider of the fates of unjust men:
She leads them a mad dance, she makes them blind
To falls they should have reckoned on beforehand.

Those countrymen who set and stretched the net
Which made the lion captive – they resemble
Resentful men, the wronged who watch and wait,
Hurt carved into their hearts as into marble.
No need for more expounding on this gospel.
Kings and lords should know and catch my drift.
The world supplies enough examples of it.

Having pronounced thus, Aesop said, 'My son,
I beseech you and all men to pray
That this country be kept clear of treason,
Justice reign, and those in authority
Stay loyal to their sovereign night and day.'
And with these words he vanished and I woke,
Then homeward through the wood my journey took.

THE HIE PRUDENCE *and wirking mervelous,*
The profound wit off God omnipotent;
Is sa perfyte and sa ingenious,
Excellent far all mannis jugement;
Forquhy to him all thing is ay present,
Rycht as it is or ony tyme sall be,
Befoir the sicht off his divinitie.

Thairfoir our saull with sensualitie
So fetterit is in presoun corporall,
We may not cleirlie understand nor se
God as he is, nor thingis celestiall.
Our mirk and deidlie corps materiale
Blindis the spirituall operatioun,
Lyke as ane man wer bundin in presoun.

In Metaphisik *Aristotell sayis*
That mannis saull is lyke ane bakkis ee,
Quhilk lurkis still, als lang as licht off day is,
And in the gloming cummis furth to fle;
Hir ene ar waik, the sone scho may not se:
Sa is our saull with fantasie opprest,
To knaw the thingis in nature manifest.

The Preaching of the Swallow

GOD'S GREAT WISDOM and his marvellous workings,
The deep insight of the Omnipotent,
Are in themselves so perfect and discerning
They far excel our merely human judgement,
All things for Him being ever present,
As they are now and at all times shall be
In the full sight of His divinity.

Because our soul, imprisoned in the body,
Is bound and fettered by the sensual
We may not clearly understand or see
God as he is, or things celestial.
Our murky, gross, death-bound material
Blindfolds the operation of the spirit
Like a prisoner shut in darkness and chained up.

In his *Metaphysics* Aristotle says
The soul of man resembles a bat's eye,
The bat that hides daylong from the sun's rays,
Then in the gloaming ventures forth to fly –
Her eyes are weak, the sun she must not see.
Soul's vision too is faulty and unsure,
Missing true things manifest in Nature.

For God is in his power infinite,
And mannis saull is febill and over-small,
Off understanding waik and unperfite
To comprehend him that contenis all;
Nane suld presume be ressoun naturall
To seirche the secreitis off the Trinitie,
Bot trow fermelie and lat all ressoun be.

Yyt nevertheles we may haif knawlegeing
Off God almychtie be his creatouris,
That he is gude, fair, wyis, and bening.
Exempill tak be thir jolie flouris,
Rycht sweit off smell and plesant off colouris,
Sum grene, sum blew, sum purpour, quhyte, and reid,
Thus distribute be gift off his godheid.

The firmament payntit with sternis cleir
From eist to west rolland in cirkill round,
And everilk planet in his proper spheir,
In moving makand harmonie and sound;
The fyre, the air, the watter and the ground –
Till understand it is aneuch, iwis,
That God in all his werkis wittie is.

Luke weill the fische that swimmis in the se;
Luke weill in eirth all kynd off bestyall;
The foulis fair, sa forcelie thay fle,
Scheddand the air with pennis grit and small;
Syne luke to man, that he maid last off all,
Lyke to his image and his similitude:
Be thir we knaw that God is fair and gude.

For God is in His power infinite,
Man's soul feeble, diminutively small,
Weak in understanding and unfit
To comprehend the One who contains all.
None should presume by their own natural
Reason to unravel the Trinity.
They should have firm faith and let reason be.

Nevertheless we may gain comprehension
Of God almighty and learn from His creatures
That He is just, good, wise and most benign.
Take, for example, the loveliness of flowers,
Their rich, sweet smells, the pleasure of their colours,
Some green, some blue, some purple, white and red –
Their variety the gift of His Godhead.

The firmament, star-stippled sheer and clear,
From east to west rolling round and round;
Every planet in its proper sphere
And motion making harmony and sound;
The fire, the air, the water and the ground –
They should suffice to demonstrate to us
The intelligence of God in all his works.

Consider well the fish that swim the sea,
Consider too the beasts that dwell on land,
Birds in their strength and beauty as they fly
Cleaving the air with large or small wingspan,
Consider then His last creation, man
Made in His image and similitude:
By these we know that God is just and good.

All creature he maid for the behufe
Off man, and to his supportatioun
Into this eirth, baith under and abufe,
In number, wecht, and dew proportioun,
The difference off tyme, and ilk seasoun
Concorddand till our opurtunitie,
As daylie be experience we may se.

The Somer with his jolie mantill grene,
With flouris fair furrit on everilk fent,
Quhilk Flora, goddes off the flouris, quene,
Hes to that lord as for his seasoun lent,
And Phebus with his goldin bemis gent
Hes purfellit and payntit plesandly,
With heit and moysture stilland from the sky.

Syne Harvest hait, quhen Ceres that goddes
Hir barnis benit hes with abundance,
And Bachus, god off wyne, renewit hes
The tume pyipis in Italie and France,
With wynis wicht and liquour off plesance,
And Copia Temporis *to fill hir horne,*
That never wes full off quheit nor uther corne.

Syne Wynter wan, quhen austerne Eolus,
God off the wynd, with blastis boreall
The grene garment off somer glorious
Hes all to-rent and revin in pecis small.
Than flouris fair faidit with froist man fall,
And birdis blyith changeis thair noitis sweit
In styll murning, neir slane with snaw and sleit.

He created all things for man's benefit,
For his subsistence and his preservation
Upon the earth, beneath it and above it,
In weight, in number and correct proportion;
Differentiating time and every season
To our advantage and convenience –
As is daily evident from experience.

Summer comes in his garment green and cheerful,
Every hem and pleating flounced with flowers,
Which Flora, queen and goddess bountiful,
Has lent that lord for his due season's hours,
And Phoebus with his golden beams and glamours
And heat and moisture hazing from the sky
Has decked and dyed with colours pleasantly.

Next then warm autumn when the goddess Ceres
Heaps the barn floors high with her abundance,
And Bacchus, god of wine, replenishes
Her casks for her in Italy and France
With heady wines and liquors that entrance;
And the plenty of the season fills that horn
Of plenty never filled with wheat or corn.

Then gloomy winter, when stern Aeolus,
God of the wind, with his bleak northern blasts
Tears open, rends and rips into small pieces
The green and glorious garment summer sports.
Now fairest flowers must fade and fall to frosts
And the nearly perished songbirds modulate
Their sweet notes to lament the snow and sleet.

Thir dalis deip with dubbis drounit is,
Baith hill and holt heillit with frostis hair,
And bewis bene ar bethit, bair off blis
Be wickit windis off the winter wair.
All wyld beistis than from the bentis bair
Drawis for dreid unto thair dennis deip,
Coucheand for cauld in coifis thame to keip.

Syne cummis Ver, quhen winter is away,
The secretar off Somer with his sell,
Quhen columbie up-keikis throw the clay,
Quhilk fleit wes befoir with froistes fell.
The mavis and the merle beginnis to mell;
The lark on loft with uther birdis smale
Than drawis furth fra derne, over doun and daill.

That samin seasoun, into ane soft morning,
Rycht blyth that bitter blastis wer ago,
Unto the wod, to se the flouris spring,
And heir the mavis sing and birdis mo,
I passit furth, syne lukit to and fro
To see the soill, that wes richt sessonabill,
Sappie, and to resave all seidis abill.

Moving thusgait, grit myrth I tuke in mynd,
Off lauboraris to se the besines,
Sum makand dyke, and sum the pleuch can wynd,
Sum sawand seidis fast frome place to place,
The harrowis hoppand in the saweris trace;
It wes grit joy to him that luifit corne
To se thame laubour, baith at evin and morne.

The dales are flooded deep with dirty puddles,
Hills and hedges covered with hoar frost,
The sheltering bough is stripped and shrinks and shudders
In cruel winds as winter does its worst.
All creatures of the wild withdraw perforce
From blasted farmlands to hole up and cower
Against the cold in burrow, den or lair.

Then when winter's gone there comes the spring –
Summer's secretary, bearing his seal –
When columbine peeps out after hiding
Her fearful head beneath the frosty field.
The thrushes and the blackbirds sing their fill.
The lark on high, soaring far up yonder,
Is seen again, and other little songsters.

That same season, one mild and pleasant morning,
Delighted that the bitter blasts were gone,
I walked in woods to see the flowers blooming
And hear the thrush and songbirds at their song,
And as I walked and looked and wandered on
Enjoyed the prospect of the vernal soil
Ready for seed, in good heart, fresh and fertile.

Free and easy like that, on I go,
Happy watching labourers at their tasks,
Some digging ditches, some behind the plough,
Some in full stride, sowing the seed broadcast,
The harrow hopping off the ground they'd paced.
For one who loved the corn crop, it was joy
To see them at their work there, late and early.

And as I baid under ane bank full bene,
In hart gritlie rejosit off that sicht,
Unto ane hedge, under ane hawthorne grene,
Off small birdis thair come ane ferlie flicht,
And doun belyif can on the leifis licht
On everilk syde about me quhair I stude,
Rycht mervellous, ane mekill multitude.

Amang the quhilks, ane swallow loud couth cry,
On that hawthorne hie in the croip sittand:
'O ye birdis on bewis heir me by,
Ye sall weill knaw and wyislie understand:
Quhair danger is, or perrell appeirand,
It is grit wisedome to provyde befoir
It to devoyd, for dreid it hurt yow moir.'

'Schir Swallow,' quod the lark agane, and leuch,
'Quhat have ye sene that causis yow to dreid?'
'Se ye yone churll', quod scho, 'beyond yone pleuch
Fast sawand hemp – lo se! – and linget seid?
Yone lint will grow in lytill tyme indeid,
And thairoff will yone churll his nettis mak,
Under the quhilk he thinkis us to tak.

'Thairfoir I reid we pas quhen he is gone
At evin, and with our naillis scharp and small
Out off the eirth scraip we yone seid anone
And eit it up, for giff it growis we sall
Have cause to weip heirefter ane and all.
Se we remeid thairfoir furthwith, instante,
Nam levius laedit quicquid praevidimus ante.

Then as I stood beneath a bank to rest,
Heartened and elated by the scene,
There swooped into the hedge in sudden haste
And quickly lit and roosted on the green
Leaves of the hawthorn bush that was my screen
A flock of small birds, everywhere at once,
Innumerable, amazing, marvellous.

Among them next I heard a swallow cry
From where she perched on the top branch of the thorn,
'You birds there on your branches, hear, O hear me,
And be instructed; understand and learn.
When dangers loom or when perils threaten
The wise course is to foresee and take care:
Plan, make provision, think, forestall and store.'

The lark laughed and then answered, 'Lady Swallow,
What have you seen that's making you afraid?'
'Do you see', she said, 'yon fellow with his plough
Sowing – look – hemp and lint, broadcasting seed?
In no time at all the lint will braird
And when it's grown that churl will make a net
And already plots to snare us under it.

'So my advice is this: when he is gone
This evening we descend and with our claws
Scrape every seed out of the earth and then
Eat it immediately, for if it grows
We'll surely rue the day – and with good cause.
Thus straightway we shall remedy our case
Since the one who takes precautions suffers less.

'For clerkis sayis it is nocht sufficient
To considder that is befoir thyne ee;
Bot prudence is ane inwart argument
That garris ane man provyde befoir and se
Quhat gude, quhat evill, is liklie for to be
Off everilk thingis at the fynall end,
And swa fra perrell the better him defend.'

The lark, lauchand, the swallow thus couth scorne,
And said scho fischit lang befoir the net –
'The barne is eith to busk that is unborne;
All growis nocht that in the ground is set;
The nek to stoup quhen it the straik sall get
Is sone aneuch; deith on the fayest fall.'
Thus scornit thay the swallow ane and all.

Despysing thus hir helthsum document,
The foulis ferlie tuke thair flicht anone:
Sum with ane bir thay braidit over the bent,
And sum agane ar to the grene wod gone.
Upon the land quhair I wes left allone
I tuke my club, and hamewart couth I carie,
Swa ferliand as I had sene ane farie.

Thus passit furth quhill June, that jolie tyde,
And seidis that wer sawin off beforne
Wer growin hie, that hairis mycht thame hyde,
And als the quailye craikand in the corne.
I movit furth betuix midday and morne
Unto the hedge under the hawthorne grene,
Quhair I befoir the said birdis had sene,

'For scholars say it is not sufficient
To consider only things that you can see,
Prudence being an inner discipline
That causes one to look ahead and be
Aware what good or evil end is likely,
Which course of action better guarantees
Our safety in the last analysis.'

The lark laughed at the swallow then for scorn
And said she fished before she'd found a net –
'The baby's easy dressed before it's born.
What grows is never all that has been set;
It's time enough to bend and bare the neck
When the blow is aimed; most fated's like to fall.'
And so they scorned the swallow, one and all.

Despising thus her salutary lesson
The birds departed in a sudden flurry;
Some whirled across the fields in quick commotion,
Some to the greenwood in a panicked hurry.
Left on my own then, out there in the country,
I took my staff and headed back for home
In wonderment, as in a waking dream.

Time passed, then came the pleasant month of June
When seeds that had been sown earlier
Grew high round corncrakes craking out their tune
And hiding places of the leaping hare.
So again one morning l went roving where
I found that same hedge and green hawthorn tree
Which held those birds I've spoken of already.

And as I stude, be aventure and cace,
The samin birdis as I haif said yow air –
I hoip because it wes thair hanting-place,
Mair off succour, or yit mair solitair –
Thay lychtit doun, and quhen thay lychtit wair,
The swallow swyth put furth ane pietuous pyme,
Said, 'Wo is him can not bewar in tyme!

'O blind birdis, and full off negligence,
Unmyndfull off your awin prosperitie,
Lift up your sicht and tak gude advertence,
Luke to the lint that growis on yone le.
Yone is the thing I bad, forsuith, that we,
Quhill it wes seid, suld rute furth off the eird;
Now is it lint, now is it hie on breird.

'Go yit, quhill it is tender, young, and small,
And pull it up, let it na mair incres.
My flesche growis, my bodie quaikis all,
Thinkand on it I may not sleip in peis!'
Thay cryit all, and bad the swallow ceis,
And said, 'Yone lint heirefter will do gude,
For linget is to lytill birdis fude.

'We think, quhen that yone lint bollis ar ryip,
To mak us feist and fill us off the seid,
Magré yone churll, and on it sing and pyip.'
'Weill,' quod the swallow, 'freindes, hardilie beid;
Do as ye will, bot certane, sair I dreid
Heirefter ye sall find als sour as sweit,
Quhen ye ar speldit on yone carlis speit.

And as I stood there, by the strangest chance,
Those same birds you have heard me talk about –
Maybe because it was one of their haunts,
A safer, maybe, or a lonelier spot –
They lighted down and when they had alit
The swallow cheeped, still harping on her theme:
'Woe to the one who won't beware in time.

'You birds, so blinded and so negligent,
Unmindful of your own prosperity,
Lift up your eyes, see clearly what has happened:
Look at the lint now growing on yon lea.
That is the stuff I argued once that we
Should uproot, while it was seed, from the earth.
Now it's a crop, young stalks, a sprouting braird.

'While it's still tender, immature, and small,
Go, stop it growing. Pull it up this minute.
It makes my heart beat fast and my flesh crawl,
It gives me nightmares just to think of it.'
The other birds then cried out and protested
And told the swallow: 'That lint will do us good.
Is linseed not our little fledglings' food?

'When the flax is grown and the seed-pods ripe
We'll feast and take our fill then of the seed,
And sing and swing on it and peep and pipe.
Who cares about the farmer?' 'So be it,'
The swallow said. 'But I am sore afraid
You'll find things bitter that now seem so sweet
When you're scorched and skewered on yon fellow's spit.

'The awner off yone lint ane fouler is,
Richt cautelous and full off subteltie;
His pray full sendill-tymis will he mis
Bot giff we birdis all the warrer be.
Full mony off our kin he hes gart de,
And thocht it bot ane sport to spill thair blude;
God keip me fra him, and the halie rude.'

Thir small birdis haveand bot lytill thocht
Off perrell that mycht fall be aventure
The counsell off the swallow set at nocht,
Bot tuke thair flicht and furth togidder fure;
Sum to the wode, sum markit to the mure.
I tuke my staff, quhen this wes said and done,
And walkit hame, for it drew neir the none.

The lynt ryipit, the carll pullit the lyne,
Rippillit the bollis, and in beitis set,
It steipit in the burne, and dryit syne,
And with ane bittill knokkit it and bet,
Syne swingillit it weill, and hekkillit in the flet;
His wyfe it span, and twynit it into threid,
Off quhilk the fowlar nettis maid indeid.

The wynter come, the wickit wind can blaw,
The woddis grene wer wallowit with the weit;
Baith firth and fell with froistys wer maid faw,
Slonkis and slaik maid slidderie with the sleit;
The foulis fair for falt thay fell off feit –
On bewis bair it wes na bute to byde,
Bot hyit unto housis thame to hyde.

'The owner of that lint field is a fowler,
A stealthy hunter, full of craft and guile,
We'll all be prey for him, birds of a feather,
Unless we watch and match him, wile for wile.
Our kith and kin he has been wont to kill:
He spilled their blood for sport, most casually.
God and his holy cross save and preserve me.'

These little birds who hardly gave a thought
To dangers that might fall by misadventure
Ignored the swallow; they set her words at nought
As they rose up and flew away together,
Some to the wood, some to the heather moor.
Noontime was approaching; I took my staff
And bearing all in mind I headed off.

The flax grew ripe, the farmer pulled it green,
Combed and dressed the seed-heads, stooked the beets,
Then buried it and steeped it in the burn,
Spread and dried it, beetled the stalks to bits,
And scutched and heckled all to tow in plaits.
His wife then spun a linen thread from it
Which the fowler took and wove into a net.

The winter came, the freezing wind did blow,
Green woods wilted in the weltering wet,
Hoar frosts hardened over hill and hollow,
Glens and gullies were slippery with sleet.
The frail and famished birds fell off their feet –
Useless to try to shelter on bare boughs,
So they hied them to the haggard and outhouses.

Sum in the barn, sum in the stak off corne
Thair lugeing tuke and maid thair residence.
The fowlar saw, and grit aithis hes sworne,
Thay suld be tane trewlie for thair expence.
His nettis hes he set with diligence,
And in the snaw he schulit hes ane plane,
And heillit it all over with calf agane.

Thir small birdis seand the calff wes glaid;
Trowand it had bene corne, thay lychtit doun,
Bot of the nettis na presume thay had,
Nor of the fowlaris fals intentioun;
To scraip and seik thair meit thay maid thame boun.
The swallow on ane lytill branche neir by,
Dreiddand for gyle, thus loud on thame couth cry:

'Into that calf scraip quhill your naillis bleid –
Thair is na corne, ye laubour all in vane.
Trow ye yone churll for pietie will yow feid?
Na, na, he hes it heir layit for ane trane.
Remove, I reid, or ellis ye will be slane.
His nettis he hes set full prively,
Reddie to draw; in tyme be war forthy!

'Grit fule is he that puttis in dangeir
His lyfe, his honour, for ane thing off nocht.
Grit fule is he that will not glaidlie heir
Counsall in tyme, quhill it availl him nocht.
Grit fule is he that hes na thing in thocht
Bot thing present, and efter quhat may fall
Nor off the end hes na memoriall.'

Some to the barn, some to the stacks of corn
Fly for shelter and settle themselves in.
The fowler sees them coming and has sworn
He'll catch and make them pay for pilfering.
He spreads his nets and in preparation
Clears a space, shovels the surface snow off,
Then tops it level with a layer of chaff.

The small birds saw the chaff and were distracted.
Believing it was corn they lighted down.
The net was the last thing they suspected.
They set to work to scrape and grub for grain
With no thought of the fowler's cunning plan.
The swallow on a little branch nearby,
Fearing a trick, shouted this warning cry:

'Scrape in that chaff until your nails are bleeding,
You're won't find any corn, no matter what.
Do you think yon churl's the sort who would be feeding
Birds out of pity? No, that chaff is bait.
I'm warning you, away, or you'll get caught.
The nets are set and ready for their prey.
Beware in time therefore, or rue the day.

'Only a fool is going to risk life
And honour on a useless enterprise;
Only a fool persists when he's warned off
And continues to ignore all good advice.
Only a fool fails to take cognisance
Of what the future holds and thinks the present
Forever stable, safe and permanent.'

Thir small birdis, for hunger famischit neir,
Full besie scraipand for to seik thair fude,
The counsall off the swallow wald not heir,
Suppois thair laubour dyd thame lytill gude.
Quhen scho thair fulische hartis understude
Sa indurate, up in ane tre scho flew –
With that this churll over thame his nettis drew.

Allace, it wes grit hartsair for to se
That bludie bowcheour beit thay birdis doun,
And for till heir, quhen thay wist weill to de,
Thair cairfull sang and lamentatioun!
Sum with ane staf he straik to eirth on swoun,
Off sum the heid he straik, off sum he brak the crag,
Sum half on lyfe he stoppit in his bag.

And quhen the swallow saw that they wer deid,
'Lo,' quod scho, 'thus it happinnis mony syis
On thame that will not tak counsall nor reid
Off prudent men or clerkis that ar wyis.
This grit perrell I tauld thame mair than thryis;
Now ar thay deid, and wo is me thairfoir!'
Scho tuke hir flicht, bot I hir saw no moir.

MORALITAS

Lo, worthie folk, Esope, that nobill clerk,
Ane poet worthie to be lawreate,
Quhen that he waikit from mair autentik werk,
With uther ma, this foirsaid fabill wrate,
Quhilk at this tyme may weill be applicate
To gude morall edificatioun,
Haifand ane sentence according to ressoun.

These little birds, half-dead from hunger now
And foraging for dear life for their food,
Paid no heed to the preaching of the swallow
Although their grubbing did them little good.
That was the moment when she understood
Their foolish hearts and minds were obdurate
And as she fled the fowler drew his net.

Alas, it was heartbreaking then to see him
Butcher those little songbirds out of hand
And hear, when they understood their hour had come,
How grievously they sang their last and mourned.
Some he hit with his stick and left there stunned,
Some he beheaded, on some he broke the neck,
Some he just stuffed alive into his sack.

And when the swallow saw that they were dead,
'Behold', she said, 'the fate that often follows
Those who won't take counsel or pay heed
To words of prudent men or wisest scholars.
Three times and more I warned them of the perils.
Now they are dead. I am saddened and heartsore.'
She flew off and I saw her then no more.

MORALITAS

Lo, worthy people, that noble scholar Aesop,
A poet worthy to be laureate,
When he relaxed from more exacting work
Wrote this fable and other fables like it
Which at this moment serve to educate
And edify, because they have a meaning
That furthers good and accords with reason.

This carll and bond, of gentrice spoliate,
Sawand this calf thir small birdis to sla,
It is the feind, quhilk fra the angelike state
Exylit is, as fals apostata,
Quhilk day and nycht weryis not for to ga,
Sawand poysoun and mony wickit thocht
In mannis saull, quhilk Christ full deir hes bocht.

And quhen the saull, as seid into the eird,
Gevis consent in delectatioun,
The wickit thocht beginnis for to breird
In deidlie sin, quhilk is dampnatioun;
Ressoun is blindit with affectioun,
And carnall lust grouis full grene and gay,
Throw consuetude hantit from day to day.

Proceding furth be use and consuetude,
The sin ryipis, and schame is set on syde;
The feynd plettis his nettis scharp and rude,
And under plesance previlie dois hyde.
Syne on the feild he sawis calf full wyde,
Quhilk is bot tume and verray vanitie
Of fleschlie lust and vaine prosperitie.

Thir hungrie birdis wretchis we may call,
Ay scraipand in this warldis vane plesance,
Greddie to gadder gudis temporall,
Quhilk as the calf ar tume without substance,
Lytill of availl and full of variance,
Lyke to the mow befoir the face of wind
Quhiskis away and makis wretchis blind.

This tenant churl, this mean ignoble peasant
Sowing chaff, making small birds his prey,
He is the fiend in exile from high heaven,
An angel cast down by the deity,
Ever unrelenting and unweary,
Apt to poison man's thought and his soul
Which Christ redeemed most dearly for us all.

And when the soul (figured as seed in earth)
Yields to the flesh and sensual temptation,
Then wickedness begins to bloom and braird
As mortal sin, which issues in damnation.
Reason is thus blindfolded by passion
And carnal lust springs green and takes deep root
Daily and deliciously through habit.

Thus practised and confirmed, habituated,
Sin ripens and all shame is cast aside.
The fiend cross-weaves and webs his cruel net
And lurks in secret under pleasure's bed.
Then on the field he sows chaff far and wide –
Lusts of the flesh, insubstantial, empty,
Will-o'-the-wisps and vacuous vanity.

These hungry birds stand for those poor wretches
Grubbing in the world for goods and gain,
Busy rooting round for earthly riches
Which, like the chaff, are insubstantial, vain,
Of no real value, fleeting, false, a bane –
As dust whipped up and whisked before the wind
Flung in poor wretches' faces makes them blind.

This swallow, quhilk eschaipit is the snair,
The halie preichour weill may signifie,
Exhortand folk to walk and ay be wair
Fra nettis of our wickit enemie,
Quha sleipis not, bot ever is reddie,
Quhen wretchis in this warldis calf dois scraip,
To draw his net, that thay may not eschaip.

Allace, quhat cair, quhat weiping is and wo,
Quhen saull and bodie partit ar in twane!
The bodie to the wormis keitching go,
The saull to fyre, to everlestand pane.
Quhat helpis than this calf, thir gudis vane,
Quhen thow art put in Luceferis bag,
And brocht to hell, and hangit be the crag?

Thir hid nettis for to persave and se,
This sarie calf wyislie to understand,
Best is bewar in maist prosperitie,
For in this warld thair is na thing lestand.
Is na man wait how lang his stait will stand,
His lyfe will lest, nor how that he sall end
Efter his deith, nor quhidder he sall wend.

Pray we thairfoir quhill we ar in this lyfe
For four thingis: the first, fra sin remufe;
The secund is to seis all weir and stryfe;
The thrid is perfite cheritie and lufe;
The feird thing is – and maist for our behufe –
That is in blis with angellis to be fallow.
And thus endis the preiching of the swallow.

This swallow, who escaped free from the snare,
May signify in turn the holy preacher
Warning his flock to watch and still beware
The wicked fiend, our cruel fowler-netter –
Devious, unsleeping, vigilant, ever
Ready as wretches scrape in the world's chaff
To draw the net and spit them on his gaff.

Alas what grief, what weeping and what woes
There will be when the body's reft from soul.
Down to the worms' kitchen body goes,
Soul to the fire, to everlasting dole.
What help's your chaff then, will your goods console
When Lucifer has you captured in his sack
And brought to hell, to hang there by the neck?

To keep these nets in mind and not lose sight
But stay on guard against this chaff, you must
Beware most when you are most fortunate
For in this world no thing is made to last;
No man knows how his own lot has been cast,
How long he'll live, what destination he
Is going to for all eternity.

Therefore let us pray while we're alive
For these four things: the first is to shun sin;
The second is to cease from war and strife;
The third to practise charity and love;
The fourth, and the most crucial, is to win
Heavenly bliss, and hence our lives to hallow.
And so concludes the preaching of the swallow.

QWHYLUM THAIR WYNNIT *in ane wildernes,*
As myne authour expreslie can declair,
Ane revand wolff, that levit upon purches
On bestiall, and maid him weill to fair;
Wes nane sa big about him he wald spair
And he war hungrie, outher for favour or feid;
Bot in his breith he weryit thame to deid.

Swa happinnit him in watching as he went
To meit ane foxe in middis off the way.
He him foirsaw, and fenyeit to be schent,
And with ane bek he bad the wolff gude day.
'Welcum to me,' quod he, 'thow Russell gray.'
Syne loutit doun, and tuke him be the hand:
'Ryse up, Lowrence! I leif the for to stand.

'Quhair hes thow bene this sesoun fra my sicht?
Thow sall beir office, and my stewart be,
For thow can knap doun caponis on the nicht,
And lourand law thow can gar hennis de.'
'Schir,' said the foxe, 'that ganis not for me;
And I am rad, gif thay me se on far,
That at my figure beist and bird will skar.'

The Fox, the Wolf and the Carter

ONCE UPON A TIME, in a wilderness
(According to the author of my tale)
There lived a wolf, a reiver ravenous
Round field and fold, freebooting in great style,
Killing, culling, plundering at will,
Showing no fear or favour: he rampaged.
The strong weren't spared. The weaker ones were savaged.

One day when he was on his usual hunt
He chanced to meet a fox upon the way.
But fox had spied him and as was his wont
Dissembled. Acted scared. Bowed. Bade good day.
'Well met,' said he, 'friend wolf.' Then down he lay
And wolf falls for it, reaches out his hand
And says, 'Sir fox! Come now. Stop cringing. Stand!

'Where have you been these ages from my sight?
We must link up. You be my agent. Be
My hen-snatcher, my roost-raider by night.
Creep into coops. Go on a fowling spree.'
'O sir,' said fox, 'that's not a job for me.
You know what happens. The minute I appear,
There's panic in each henhouse, pen and byre.'

'Na,' quod the wolff, 'thow can in covert creip
Upon thy wame and hint thame be the heid,
And mak ane suddand schow upon ane scheip,
Syne with thy wappinnis wirrie him to deid.'
'Schir,' said the foxe, 'ye knaw my roib is reid,
And thairfoir thair will na beist abyde me,
Thocht I wald be sa fals as for to hyde me.'

'Yis,' quod the wolff, 'throw buskis and throw brais
Law can thow lour to come to thy intent.'
'Schir,' said the foxe, 'ye wait weill how it gais;
Ane lang space fra thame thay will feill my sent.
Than will thay eschaip, suppois I suld be schent;
And I am schamefull for to cum behind thame,
Into the feild thocht I suld sleipand find thame.'

'Na,' quod the wolff, 'thow can cum on the wind;
For everie wrink, forsuith, thow hes ane wyle.'
'Schir,' said the foxe, 'that beist ye mycht call blind
That micht not eschaip than fra me ane myle:
How micht I ane off thame that wyis begyle?
My tippit twa eiris and my twa gray ene
Garris me be kend quhair I wes never sene.'

Than said the wolff, 'Lowrence, I heir the le,
And castys for perrellis thy ginnes to defend;
Bot all thy sonyeis sall not availl the,
About the busk with wayis thocht thow wend.
Falset will failye ay at the latter end:
To bow at bidding and byde not quhill thow brest,
Thairfoir I giff the counsall for the best.'

'No,' cries the wolf. 'Not so. For you can creep
Low on your knees and nab hens by the head,
Can make a sudden tackle on a sheep,
Then shake and rake and rack him till he's dead.'
'Sir,' says the fox, 'you know my coat is red
And so well watched, in spite of all my cunning
There's not a beast now doesn't see me coming.'

'Still,' said the wolf, 'by brakes and braes you wend
And slink along and steal up on your prey.'
'Sir,' said the fox, 'you know how these things end.
They catch my scent downwind from far away
And scatter fast and leave me in dismay.
They could be lying sleeping in a field
But once I'm close they're off. It puts me wild.'

'But', cried the wolf, 'you can come down upwind.
For every trick they work you have a wile.'
'Sir,' said the fox, 'no beast that isn't blind
But could escape from me by many a mile.
How can I fend when all my old schemes fail?
These pointed ears! These two grey eyes! I'm known
Before I'm seen at all. My cover's gone.'

'Oh,' cried the wolf, 'I fear you tell a lie.
You weave and dodge to keep your secrets safe.
You beat about the bush. You're far too sly.
But nothing you can say will put me off.
Lies and false trails won't give you the last laugh
So listen well to what I'm saying to you:
Do what you're bid. Obey before you're made to.'

'Schir,' said the foxe, 'it is Lentring, ye se;
I can nocht fische, for weiting off my feit,
To tak ane banestikill, thocht we baith suld de;
I have nane uther craft to win my meit.
Bot wer it Pasche, that men suld pultrie eit,
As kiddis, lambis, or caponis into ply,
To beir your office than wald I not set by.'

Than said the wolff in wraith, 'Wenis thou with wylis
And with thy mony mowis me to mat?
It is ane auld dog, doutles, that thow begylis;
Thow wenis to drau the stra befoir the cat!'
'Schir,' said the foxe, 'God wait, I mene not that;
For and I did, it wer weill worth that ye
In ane reid raip had tyit me till ane tre.

'Bot nou I se he is ane fule perfay
That with his maister fallis in ressoning.
I did bot till assay quhat ye wald say;
God wait, my mynd wes on ane uther thing.
I sall fulfill in all thing your bidding,
Quhatever ye charge on nichtis or on dayis.'
'Weill,' quod the wolff, 'I heir weill quhat thou sayis.

'Bot yit I will thow mak to me ane aith
For to be leill attour all levand leid.'
'Schir,' said the foxe, 'that ane word maks me wraith,
For nou I se ye have me at ane dreid:
Yit sall I sweir, suppois it be nocht neid,
Be Juppiter, and on pane off my heid,
I sall be treu to you quhill I be deid.'

'Sir,' said the fox, 'it's Lent, you understand,
And I can't fish. I dare not wet my feet.
I'm starved for a stickleback, for here on land
There's not a thing that you or I can eat.
But when Easter comes, when red meat and white meat
Fall off the bone, when kid and lamb and hen
Turn on the spits, I'll be your agent then.'

'So,' said the wolf in rage, 'you think you can
Get round me still? Am I wet behind the ears?
I'm far too old for all this carry-on.
Where do you think I've been these thirty years?'
'Sir,' said the fox, 'for God's sake, calm your fears.
You're so far wrong, you don't make any sense:
I could hang myself to prove my innocence.

'But now I see how foolish I have been.
No man should ever argue with his boss.
I was playing games. In no way did I mean
To give offence. So please, sir, don't be cross.
I'm at your service now and will take orders
At any time, wherever, night or day.'
'Well,' cried the wolf, 'I like well what you say,

'But even so, you'll have to swear an oath
To be true to me and put me always first.'
'Fie,' cried the fox, 'what's this? You doubt my faith?
Your suspicions are an insult. I protest!
And yet, all right, to set your mind at rest
I swear by Jupiter, on pain of death,
I'll keep my word to you while I draw breath.'

With that ane cadgear, with capill and with creillis,
Come carpand furth; than Lowrence culd him spy.
The foxe the flewer off the fresche hering feillis,
And to the wolff he roundis prively:
'Schir, yone ar hering the cadgear caryis by;
Thairfoir I reid that we se for sum wayis
To get sum fische aganis thir fasting dayis.

'Sen I am stewart, I wald we had sum stuff,
And ye ar silver-seik, I wait richt weill.
Thocht we wald thig yone verray churlische chuff,
He will not giff us ane hering off his creill –
Befoir yone churle on kneis thocht we wald kneill.
Bot yit I trou alsone that ye sall se
Giff I can craft to bleir yone carlis ee.

'Schir, ane thing is, and we get off yone pelff,
Ye man tak travell and mak us sum supplé;
For he that will not laubour and help himselff,
Into thir dayis he is not worth ane fle.
I think to work als besie as ane be –
And ye sall follou ane lytill efterwart
And gadder hering, for that sall be your part.'

With that he kest ane cumpas far about,
And straucht him doun in middis off the way;
As he wer deid he fenyeit him, but dout,
And than upon lenth unliklie lay.
The quhyte he turnit up off his ene tuay,
His toung out hang ane handbreid off his heid,
And still he lay, als straucht as he wer deid.

With that a carter with his cart and creels
Came rattling along, and fox took note.
A whiff of herring hit him in the nostrils
And he whispers to the wolf, 'Can you smell that?
It's herring that your man has in that cart
So my advice is this: we study ways
To lay in fish to tide us through fast days.

'Now I'm your agent, I have to find supplies
But you don't have two brass pence to rub together,
And if I begged and went down on my knees
On all fours here before him in the gutter
Yon gobshite wouldn't hand one herring over.
But still, no matter, wait a while and see:
I'll put one over on him presently.

'The thing is this: if we're to rip him off
You'll have to lend a hand and take a chance
For the man who's not prepared to make a move
To help himself I must discountenance.
I intend to go to work now all at once.
All you need do is walk behind the cart
And lift the herring. Thus each will play his part.'

With that he made a far, free-ranging detour,
Then stretched out in the middle of the road
Pretending to be dead, and making sure
He looked it, that the whites of his eyes showed
Like one who'd perished there for want of food.
His tongue lolled out a hand's breadth from his head
As he lay stiff and still. Perfectly dead.

The cadgear fand the foxe, and he wes fane,
And till himself thus softlie can he say:
'At the nixt bait, in faith, ye sall be flane,
And off your skyn I sall mak mittenis tway.'
He lap full lichtlie about him quhair he lay,
And all the trace he trippit on his tais;
As he had hard ane pyper play he gais.

'Heir lyis the deuyll', quod he, 'deid in ane dyke;
Sic ane selcouth sau I not this sevin yeir.
I trou ye have bene tussillit with sum tyke,
That garris you ly sa still withoutin steir.
Schir Foxe, in faith, ye ar deir welcum heir;
It is sum wyfis malisone, I trow,
For pultrie pyking, that lychtit hes on yow.

'Thair sall na pedder, for purs, nor yit for glufis,
Nor yit for poyntis, pyke your pellet fra me:
I sall off it mak mittenis to my lufis
Till hald my handis hait quhairever I be;
Till Flanderis sall it never saill the se.'
With that in hy he hint him be the heillis,
And with ane swak he swang him on the creillis,

Syne be the heid the hors in hy hes hint.
The fraudfull foxe thairto gude tent hes tane,
And with his teith the stoppell, or he stint,
Pullit out, and syne the hering ane and ane
Out off the creillis he swakkit doun gude wane.
The wolff wes war, and gadderit spedilie:
The cadgear sang, 'Huntis up, up', upon hie.

The carter found the fox and he was glad,
Boasting to himself what he would do:
'At the next stop, I'll have the fellow flayed
And fox-skin mittens cut.' Then heel and toe
He danced a dance as lightsome as a doe
As if he'd heard a piper playing reels.
Then paused and gazed and hunkered on his heels.

'Here lies', he said, 'the devil in the ditch.
I've never seen the like of it before.
Some mongrel mangled you and made dispatch
And sank you in that sleep where you don't snore.
So, Sir Fox, you are all the welcomer.
Some housewife's curse, some malison, I fear,
For raiding roosts has lighted on you here.

'No pedlar's going to purchase you. Your pelt
Won't make him gloves or trimmings or a purse.
I'm going to keep a hold of it myself
And cut and sew it into hand-warmers.
It won't be shipped across the sea to Flanders.'
And there and then he grabbed the fox's heels
And landed him high up among the creels.

Then cheerfully he takes the horse's head.
The wily fox takes heed and has begun
To bite the plug and loosen and unload
Herring from the creel-mouth, one by one,
A shoal of them, a fish-slide pouring down.
The wolf keeps close and gathers them at speed.
The carter sings 'Halloo' right long and loud.

Yit at ane burne the cadgear lukit about;
With that the foxe lap quyte the creillis fray.
The cadgear wald have raucht the foxe ane rout,
Bot all for nocht, he wan his hoill that day.
Than with ane schout thus can the cadgear say:
'Abyde, and thou ane nekhering sall haif
Is worth my capill, creillis, and all the laif.'

'Now,' quod the foxe, 'I schreu me and we meit!
I hard quhat thou hecht to do with my skyn.
Thy handis sall never in thay mittinnis tak heit,
And thou wer hangit, carll, and all thy kyn!
Do furth thy mercat – at me thou sall nocht wyn –
And sell thy hering thou hes thair till hie price;
Ellis thow sall wyn nocht on thy merchandice.'

The cadgear trimmillit for teyne quhair that he stude.
'It is weill worthie', quod he, 'I want yone tyke,
That had nocht in my hand sa mekill gude
As staff or sting yone truker for to stryke.'
With that lychtlie he lap out over ane dyke
And snakkit doun ane staff – for he wes tene –
That hevie wes and off the holyne grene.

With that the foxe unto the wolff could wend,
And fand him be the hering quhair he lyis.
'Schir,' said he than, 'maid I not fair defend?
Ane wicht man wantit never, and he wer wyis;
Ane hardie hart is hard for to suppryis.'
Than said the wolff, 'Thow art ane berne full bald,
And wyse at will, in gude tyme be it tald.

But at a burn he turns and looks about.
The fox leaps clear and legs it from the creels.
The carter would have hit a deadly clout
But fox has shown a clean pair of heels
And headed for his den. Then carter howls:
'A gutting I'll give you, a herring-treat,
A second helping that you'll not forget.'

'Be damned,' the fox said, 'for we'll never meet.
I heard you planning how you'd use my skin.
Your hands will never feel those mittens' heat.
God's curse you, hellion, you and all your kin.
Go sell your goods. I won't be in the bargain.
Sell herring at the highest price you can –
Whatever herring's left. Farewell, fishman!'

The carter shook with anger where he stood.
'It serves me right,' he said, 'I missed the cur.
I should have had a staff of seasoned wood
To hammer him and break his sleekit shoulder.'
With that he faced the ditch and vaulted over
And hacked himself a staff and dressed it clean,
A heavy, hard, straight stick of holly green.

Off went the fox then to his boss accomplice
And found him by the herring, standing guard.
'Sir,' said the fox, 'can I not pierce defences
Sylishly and well? It is always hard
To keep a brave man from his just reward.'
The wolf agreed. He said, 'I do confess
You're ever capable and brave and wise.

'Bot quhat wes yone the carll cryit on hie,
And schuke his hand?' quod he. 'Hes thou no feill?'
'Schir,' said the foxe, 'that I can tell trewlie;
He said the nekhering wes intill the creill.'
'Kennis thou that hering?' 'Ye, schir, I ken it weill,
And at the creill mouth I had it thryis but dout:
The wecht off it neir tit my tuskis out.

'Now suithlie, schir, micht we that hering fang,
It wald be fische to us thir fourtie dayis.'
Than said the wolff, 'Nou God nor that I hang!
Bot to be thair I wald gif all my clays,
To se gif that my wappinnis mycht it rais.'
'Schir,' said the foxe, 'God wait, I wischit you oft,
Quhen that my pith micht not beir it on loft.

'It is ane syde off salmond, as it wair,
And callour, pypand lyke ane pertrik ee:
It is worth all the hering ye have thair --
Ye, and we had it swa, is it worth sic thre.'
Than said the wolff, 'Quhat counsell gevis thou me?'
'Schir,' said the foxe, 'wirk efter my devyis,
And ye sall have it, and tak you na suppryis.

'First, ye man cast ane cumpas far about,
Syne straucht you doun in middis off the way;
Baith heid and feit and taill ye man streik out,
Hing furth your toung, and clois weill your ene tway,
Syne se your heid on ane hard place ye lay;
And doubt not for na perrell may appeir,
Bot hald you clois, quhen that the carll cummis neir.

'But what', he went on, 'was that idiot shouting
When he hunted you and howled and shook his fist?'
'Sir,' said the fox, 'his words are worth repeating.
A herring treat, he mocked me, I had missed.
A second helping that I'd never taste.'
'And was there such a treat?' 'There was. I'd caught it
But it weighed too much and nearly tore my teeth out.

'But truly, boss, if we could land that catch
It would see us through our forty days of fast.'
Then wolf said, 'I will risk it. We must fetch
That Lent-feed here. My strong teeth can lay waste
To herring-bone and basket-work, I trust.'
'Indeed,' the fox replied, 'I often wished
For your bite and brawn to help me raise that fish.

'It's like a side of salmon, more or less,
Shiny as a partridge eye, and luscious –
Worth more than all those herring on the grass,
Three times as tasty, three times more precious.'
'Then,' cried the wolf, 'advise me on my course.'
'Sir,' said the fox, 'keep strictly to my plan
And all being well, we will outwit our man.

'First you must make a far, free-ranging detour,
Then stretch down in the middle of the road
With head and feet and tail out, making sure
Your tongue is lolling and your two eyes closed.
Then find a hard support to hold your head
And ignoring every threat that may appear,
Stay motionless until the coof comes near.

'And thocht ye se ane staf, have ye na dout,
Bot hald you wonder still into that steid;
And luke your ene be clois, as thay wer out,
And se that ye schrink nouther fute nor heid:
Than will the cadgear carll trou ye be deid,
And intill haist will hint you be the heillis,
As he did me, and swak you on his creillis.'

'Now,' quod the wolff, 'I sweir the be my thrift,
I trou yone cadgear carll dow not me beir.'
'Schir,' said the foxe, 'on loft he will you lift
Upon his creillis, and do him lytill deir –
Bot ane thing dar I suithlie to you sweir:
Get ye that hering sicker in sum place,
Ye sall not fair in fisching mair quhill Pasche.

'I sall say In principio upon yow,
And crose your corps from the top to tay;
Wend quhen ye will, I dar be warrand now
That ye sall de na suddand deith this day.'
With that the wolff gird up sone and to gay,
And caist ane cumpas about the cadgear far;
Syne raucht him in the gait, or he come nar.

He laid his halfheid sicker hard and sad,
Syne straucht his four feit fra him, and his heid,
And hang his toung furth as the foxe him bad;
Als styll he lay as he wer verray deid,
Rakkand nathing off the carlis favour nor feid,
Bot ever upon the nekhering he thinkis,
And quyte foryettis the foxe and all his wrinkis.

'And though you see a staff, continue quiet.
Don't move a muscle and don't be afraid.
Keep eyes tight closed as though they'd been put out.
Don't shrink at knee or neck or foot or head.
That carter clown will imagine you are dead
And quickly lug and lift you by the heels
As he did me, and fling you on the creels.'

'But wait,' the wolf says, 'for as sure as God
I'll be too weighty for the coof to lift.'
'Sir,' said the fox, 'he is a hefty bawd.
One heave and you'll be high and dry aloft.
But this much I can guarantee you: if
You haul that herring safely out of there,
You needn't fish again till Lent next year.

I now say *in principio* and pray
A blessing on your body, head to toe,
Which means henceforth you travel on your way
Protected against death. God speed you. Go!'
Up springs the wolf then and away out through
The gaps and gates, detouring to avoid
The fishman coming up along the road.

He makes a sturdy pillow of a stone,
Then stretches out his four feet and his head,
Lets his tongue loll and settles himself down,
Just as the fox instructed, to feign dead.
He's over any fear he might have had.
The only thing he thinks is 'herring-treat'.
The last thing on his mind is fox-deceit.

With that the cadgear, als wraith as ony wind,
Come rydand on the laid, for it wes licht,
Thinkand ay on the foxe that wes behind,
Upon quhat wyse revengit on him he micht;
And at the last of the wolff gat ane sicht,
Quhair he in lenth lay streikit in the gait –
Bot giff he lichtit doun or nocht, God wait!

Softlie he said, 'I wes begylit anis;
Be I begylit twyis, I schrew us baith!
That evill bat it sall licht upon thy banis
He suld have had that hes done me the skaith.'
On hicht he hovit the staf, for he wes wraith,
And hit him with sic will upon the heid
Quhill neir he swonit and swelt into that steid.

Thre battis he bure, or he his feit micht find,
Bot yit the wolff wes wicht, and wan away;
He mycht not se – he wes sa verray blind –
Nor wit reddilie quhether it wes nicht or day.
The foxe beheld that service quhair he lay,
And leuch on loft quhen he the wolff sa seis,
Baith deif and dosinnit, fall swonand on his kneis.

He that of ressoun can not be content,
Bot covetis all, is abill all to tyne.
The foxe, quhen that he saw the wolff wes schent,
Said to himself, 'Thir hering sall be myne.'
I le, or ellis he wes a stewart fyne,
That fand sic wayis his maister for to greif.
With all the fische thus Lowrence tuke his leif.

Along the carter comes then, riding high
Now that the load is lighter, in a rage
That fox had fooled him and had got away,
Mad to his get own back. At which stage
The wolf comes into view, at his old dodge,
Stiffly stretched in the middle of the road.
The carter (you'll have guessed) jumps off the load.

Under his breath he swears, 'I was tricked once.
Be damned if I am going to be again.
The hammering I'll give you in your bones
Your friend should have been given first time round.'
With that he lifts the holly in his hand
And comes down with such force upon his head
The wolf convulsed and very nearly died.

Three blows he bore before he found his feet
And though he still was strong enough to flee
The blows had blinded him: he had been hit
So hard he hardly saw the light of day.
The fox, who watched it all from where he lay,
Laughed long and loud at wolf-who-would-be-boss
Brought to his knees, two-double, in collapse.

Thus one who's not content with what's enough
But covets all deserves to forfeit all.
The fox, when he saw the sad rout of the wolf,
Thought 'Herring-treat!' and then 'A bellyful!'
It takes, you will agree, both neck and skill
To teach a boss what's honour among thieves.
The fox secures his herring-hoard and leaves.

The wolff wes neir weill dungin to the deid,
That uneith with his lyfe away he wan,
For with the bastoun weill brokin wes his heid.
The foxe into his den sone drew him than,
That had betraisit his maister and the man:
The ane wantit the hering off his creillis;
The utheris blude wes rynnand over his heillis.

MORALITAS

This taill is myngit with moralitie,
As I sall schaw sumquhat, or that I ceis.
The foxe unto the warld may likkinnit be;
The revand wolf unto ane man, but leis;
The cadgear, deith, quhome under all man preis –
That ever tuke lyfe throw cours of kynd man dee,
As man, and beist, and fische into the see.

The warld, ye wait, is stewart to the man,
Quhilk makis man to haif na mynd of deid,
Bot settis for winning all the craftis thay can.
The hering I likkin unto the gold sa reid,
Quhilk gart the wolf in perrell put his heid –
Richt swa the gold garris landis and cieteis
With weir be waistit daylie, as men seis.

And as the foxe with dissimulance and gyle
Gart the wolf wene to haif worschip for ever,
Richt swa this warld with vane glore for ane quhyle
Flatteris with folk as thay suld failye never;
Yit suddandlie men seis it oft dissever;
With thame that trowis oft to fill the sek,
Deith cummis behind and nippis thame be the neck.

The wolf was lucky to escape alive.
He had been so unmercifully beaten
He limped and could no longer roam nor reive.
The fox slipped off downwind back to his den,
Glad to have duped his master and the man:
The one was missing herring from his creels,
The other losing ground, blood to the heels.

MORALITAS

This story happens to contain a moral
Which in conclusion I must underline.
The fox may be compared unto the World,
The robber wolf most definitely to Man
And the fish-carter to Death, our mortal bane,
Since all that lives in nature has to die –
On earth or under earth, in sea or sky.

Man has the world as servant; and the world
Makes him forget that one day he'll be dead.
It sets his mind on wealth, it turns his head,
So in my tale the herring means this greed
For goods and gain the wolf exhibited.
Greed and plunder, war and devastation
Are still the wolf's rampage in every nation.

The fox with plausibility and guile
Gulled the wolf into false security.
Just so the world gulls people for a while.
They credit their newfound prosperity
Only to see it lost as suddenly.
They burgle time and fill their sack with things
But death will dog their heels and cut their hamstrings.

The micht of gold makis mony men sa blind,
That settis on avarice thair felicitie,
That thay foryet the cadgear cummis behind
To stryke thame, of quhat stait sa ever thay be:
Quhat is mair dirk than blind prosperitie?
Quhairfoir, I counsell mychtie men to haif mynd
Of the nekhering, interpreit in this kynd.

The drive to own possessions makes men blind.
Avarice rampant is renamed success.
But they forget the carter comes behind
To spoil the sport and void what they invest.
The hollow of the wave follows the crest.
I therefore counsel all concerned: remember
Carter, fox and wolf, and what they stand for.

IN ELDERIS DAYIS, as Esope can declair,
Thair wes ane husband quhilk had ane plewch to steir.
His use wes ay in morning to ryse air:
Sa happinnit him, in streiking tyme off yeir,
Airlie in the morning to follou furth his feir
Unto the pleuch, bot his gadman and he.
His stottis he straucht with 'Benedicite!';

The caller cryit, 'How! Haik!' upon hicht,
'Hald draucht, my dowis!' Syne broddit thame full sair:
The oxin wes unusit, young, and licht,
And for fersnes thay couth the fur forfair.
The husband than woxe angrie as ane hair,
Syne cryit, and caist his patill and grit stanis:
'The wolff', quod he, 'mot have you all at anis!'

Bot yit the wolff wes neirar nor he wend,
For in ane busk he lay, and Lowrence baith,
In ane rouch rone wes at the furris end,
And hard the hecht; than Lowrence leuch full raith:
'To tak yone bud,' quod he, 'it wer na skaith.'
'Weill,' quod the wolff, 'I hecht the, be my hand,
Yone carlis word as he wer king sall stand.'

The Fox, the Wolf and the Farmer

IN OLDEN DAYS, as Aesop has recorded,
There was a farmer wont to speed the plough.
Early rising ever was his habit
And so, come ploughing time, he rose to go
Early afield to open the first furrow,
His farmhand with him, leading out the oxen.
He blessed himself and them, and started in.

The farmhand shouted, 'Top it up! Come on!
Pull straight, my pets!' Then flailed them hard and sore.
The team was fresh and young and barely broken,
So hard to rein they wrecked the new-ploughed score.
The farmer let a sudden angry roar,
Stoned them, threw down the pattle of the plough.
'The wolf', he yelled, 'can have the lot of you.'

But yet the wolf was nearer than he knew
For he lay with Mr Fox in a bush nearby,
A thicket at the far end of the furrow,
And heard the vow. Fox laughed in quick reply:
'Now there's an offer', he told wolf, 'which I
Consider good.' 'I promise you,' wolf answered,
'I'll make yon royal clown stand by his word.'

The oxin waxit mair reulie at the last;
Syne efter they lousit, fra that it worthit weill lait.
The husband hamewart with his cattell past.
Than sone the wolff come hirpilland in his gait
Befoir the oxin, and schupe to mak debait.
The husband saw him, and worthit sumdeill agast,
And bakwart with his beistis wald haif past.

The wolff said, 'Quhether dryvis thou this pray?
I chalenge it, for nane off thame ar thyne!'
The man thairoff wes in ane felloun fray,
And soberlie to the wolff answerit syne:
'Schir, be my saull, thir oxin ar all myne:
Thairfoir I studdie quhy ye suld stop me,
Sen that I faltit never to you, trewlie.'

The wolff said, 'Carll, gaif thou not me this drift
Airlie, quhen thou wes eirrand on yone bank?
And is thair oucht, sayis thou, frear than gift?
This tarying wyll tyne the all thy thank:
Far better is frelie for to giff ane plank
Nor be compellit on force to giff ane mart.
Fy on the fredome that cummis not with hart!'

'Schir,' quod the husband, 'ane man may say in greif,
And syne ganesay fra he avise and se.
I hecht to steill; am I thairfoir ane theif?
God forbid, schir, all hechtis suld haldin be.
Gaif I my hand or oblissing,' quod he,
'Or have ye witnes or writ for to schau?
Schir, reif me not, bot go and seik the lau.'

Finally the oxen settled down.
Then, later on, the two men unyoked them.
The farmer with his team set off for home.
The wolf straightway limped out and came loping
Into their path to work his stratagem.
The farmer saw him, couldn't but take fright,
And thought to turn the beasts and make retreat.

'Where are you going with this stolen stock,'
The wolf laid claim, 'for none of them are yours?'
The man, although now thrown into panic,
Faces the wolf and deliberately answers,
'Sir, by my soul, all of these oxen-steers
Are mine. I am puzzled that you stop me.
For never once did I offend you. Truly.'

The wolf said, 'Fellow, did you not just now
Donate them to me as you ploughed yon bank?
And is there any finer deed, I ask you,
Than a free deed of gift? You forfeit thanks
By stalling. Better liberal with your halfpence
Than forced in the end to part with fatted stock.
Generosity not from the heart is mock.'

'Sir,' said the farmer, 'a man may speak in fury
And then gainsay himself once he's considered.
If I say I'll steal, does it make a thief of me?
Do promises like that have to be honoured?
Did I sign documents? Or give my word?
What writ or witness do you have to show?
Do not, sir, seek to rob me. Go to law.'

'Carll,' quod the wolff, 'ane lord, and he be leill,
That schrinkis for schame, or doutis to be repruvit –
His sau is ay als sickker as his seill.
Fy on the leid that is not leill and lufit!
Thy argument is fals, and eik contrufit,
For it is said in proverb: "But lawté
All uther vertewis ar nocht worth ane fle." '

'Schir,' said the husband, 'remember of this thing:
Ane leill man is not tane at halff ane taill.
I may say and ganesay; I am na king.
Quhair is your witnes that hard I hecht thame haill?'
Than said the wolff, 'Thairfoir it sall nocht faill.
Lowrence,' quod he, 'cum hidder of that schaw,
And say nathing bot as thow hard and saw.'

Lowrence come lourand, for he lufit never licht,
And sone appeirit befoir thame in that place:
The man leuch nathing quhen he saw that sicht.
'Lowrence,' quod the wolff, 'thow man declair this cace,
Quhairof we sall schaw the suith in schort space.
I callit on the leill witnes for to beir:
Quhat hard thou that this man hecht me lang eir?'

'Schir,' said the tod, 'I can not hastelie
Swa sone as now gif sentence finall;
Bot wald ye baith submit yow heir to me,
To stand at my decreit perpetuall,
To pleis baith I suld preif, gif it may fall.'
'Weill,' quod the wolff, 'I am content for me.'
The man said, 'Swa am I, however it be.'

'Clown,' said the wolf, 'a lord, if he is honest
And lives in fear of shame and of reproof,
His word alone will be his seal of trust.
Fie on the man we can't believe or have
Respect for. You're contriving to deceive,
And without honesty, the proverbs say,
Other virtues are flimsy as a fly.'

'Sir,' said the farmer, 'remember this one thing.
An honest man's not tricked by a half-truth.
I may say and gainsay, I am no king,
But where's the witness you can put on oath?'
Then said the wolf, 'Let you take him on good faith.
Lawrence,' he calls, 'come here out of that covert,
And say exactly what you saw and heard.'

Lawrence came lurking – he never loved the light –
And soon appeared before them in that place.
The man saw nothing in the sight to laugh at.
'Lawrence,' said wolf, 'you must decide this case,
The truth of which we'll demonstrate with ease.
I call for honest witness: in his wrath,
What gift did this man promise I would have?'

'Sir,' said the fox, 'a final verdict now
Would be premature and unduly hasty,
But if you would submit, the pair of you,
To what I rule in perpetuity
I'll do my best to judge the case as fairly
As can be done.' 'Well,' said the wolf, 'agreed.'
And the man said, 'Yes, again agreed.'

Than schew thay furth thair allegeance but fabill,
And baith proponit thair pley to him compleit.
Quod Lowrence, 'Now I am ane juge amycabill:
Ye sall be sworne to stand at my decreit,
Quhether heirefter ye think it soure or sweit.'
The wolff braid furth his fute, the man his hand,
And on the toddis taill sworne thay ar to stand.

Than tuke the tod the man furth till ane syde,
And said him, 'Freind, thou art in blunder brocht;
The wolff will not forgif the ane oxe hyde.
Yit wald myself fane help the, and I mocht,
Bot I am laith to hurt my conscience ocht.
Tyne nocht thy querrell in thy awin defence;
This will not throu but grit coist and expence.

'Seis thou not buddis beiris bernis throw,
And giftis garris crukit materis hald full evin?
Sumtymis ane hen haldis ane man in ane kow;
All ar not halie that heifis thair handis to hevin.'
'Schir,' said the man, 'ye sall have sex or sevin
Richt off the fattest hennis off all the floik –
I compt not all the laif, leif me the coik.'

'I am ane juge,' quod Lowrence than, and leuch:
'Thair is na buddis suld beir me by the rycht.
I may tak hennis and caponis weill aneuch,
For God is gane to sleip, as for this nycht;
Sic small thingis ar not sene into his sicht.
Thir hennis', quod he, 'sall mak thy querrell sure:
With emptie hand na man suld halkis lure.'

Both then made their allegations frankly,
Both sets of pleas set forth by them complete.
'Though I act as judge in friendship, you must be
Bound', said Lawrence, 'to accept my verdict
However it may strike you, sour or sweet.'
The wolf stretched out his foot, the man his hand,
And swore on the fox's tail their pact would stand.

The fox then took the man off to one side
And, 'Friend,' he said, 'you're landed in a mess.
This wolf won't let you off a single oxhide
And while I myself would wish to lend assistance
I am very loath to act against my conscience.
You'll spoil your case if you make your own defence.
This can't be won without some real expense.

'You see how bribes work best to get men through
And how, for gifts, the crooked path will straighten?
Sometimes a hen will save a man a cow.
All are not holy who hoist their hands to heaven.'
'Sir,' said the man, 'you shall have six or seven
Of the very fattest hens out of my flock.
There'll be enough left if you leave the cock.'

'Now I am a judge,' said the fox and laughed,
'Bribes should not divert me from doing right.
Yet hens and capons I may well bear off
For God is gone to sleep, at least this night.
Such carry-on is petty in his sight.
These hens', he said, 'will make your case secure.
No man draws hawk to hand without a lure.'

Concordit thus, than Lowrence tuke his leiff,
And to the wolff he went into ane ling;
Syne prevelie he plukkit him be the sleiff:
'Is this in ernist', quod he, 'ye ask sic thing?
Na, be my saull, I trow it be in heithing.'
Than said the wolff, 'Lowrence, quhy sayis thou sa?
Thow hard the hecht thyselff that he couth ma.'

'The hecht', quod he, 'yone man maid at the pleuch –
Is that the cause quhy ye the cattell craif?'
Halff into heithing said Lowrence than, and leuch:
'Schir, be the rude, unroikit now ye raif:
The devill ane stirk taill thairfoir sall ye haif!
Wald I tak it upon my conscience
To do sa pure ane man as yone offence?

'Yit haif I commonnit with the carll,' quod he.
'We ar concordit upon this cunnand:
Quyte off all clamis, swa ye will mak him fre,
Ye sall ane cabok have into your hand
That sic ane sall not be in all this land,
For it is somer cheis, baith fresche and fair:
He sayis it weyis ane stane and sumdeill mair.'

'Is that thy counsell,' quod the wolff, 'I do,
That yone carll for ane cabok suld be fre?'
'Ye, be my saull, and I wer sworne yow to,
Ye suld nane uther counsell have for me;
For gang ye to the maist extremitie,
It will not wyn yow worth ane widderit neip:
Schir, trow ye not I have ane saull to keip?'

With these things settled, Lawrence took his leave,
Then went immediately to see the wolf
And there in private plucked him by the sleeve.
'Are you in earnest', he asks, 'as a plaintiff?
No, by my soul, you can't be. It's a laugh.'
'What, Lawrence, do you mean?' the wolf replied.
'You heard yourself the promise that he made.'

'The promise, is it, the man made at the plough?
Is that what you would base your case upon?'
Half-mocking like this Lawrence gave a laugh
And 'Sir, by the rood,' says he, 'your head is gone.
Devil an oxtail are you going to win!
And tricking a poor man? Who has no defence?
How could I bear to have that on my conscience?

'But I've consulted with the soul,' said he,
'And we agreed upon this covenant:
You cancel all your claims and set him free
And you'll be given, whole into your hand,
A cheese unparalleled in all the land.
He says it weighs a stone and maybe more.
It's summer cheese. Fresh. Nothing lovelier.'

'So you're advising this is what I do –
Accept the cheese so that clown can go free?'
'Yes, by my soul, and were I counsel for you
It's what I would advise professionally.
For even pushed to its extremity
Your case won't win a turnip in return.
Nor do I, sir, intend my soul to burn.'

'Weill,' quod the wolff, 'it is aganis my will
That yone carll for ane cabok suld ga quyte.'
'Schir,' quod the tod, 'ye tak it in nane evill,
For, be my saull, yourself had all the wyte.'
Than said the wolff, 'I bid na mair to flyte,
Bot I wald se yone cabok off sic pryis.'
'Schir,' said the tod, 'he tauld me quhair it lyis.'

Than hand in hand thay held unto ane hill;
The husband till his hous hes tane the way,
For he wes fane he schaippit from thair ill,
And on his feit woke the dure quhill day.
Now will we turne unto the uther tway:
Throw woddis waist thir freikis on fute can fair,
Fra busk to busk, quhill neir midnycht and mair.

Lowrence wes ever remembring upon wrinkis
And subtelteis, the wolff for to begyle;
That he had hecht ane caboik he forthinkis;
Yit at the last he findis furth ane wyle,
Than at himselff softlie couth he smyle.
The wolff sayis, 'Lowrence, thou playis bellie-blind;
We seik all nycht, bot nathing can we find.'

'Schir,' said the tod, 'we ar at it almaist;
Soft yow ane lytill, and ye sall se it sone.'
Than to ane manure-place thay hyit in haist;
The nycht wes lycht, and pennyfull the mone.
Than till ane draw-well thir senyeours past but hone,
Quhair that twa bukkettis severall suithlie hang;
As ane come up ane uther doun wald gang.

'Well,' said the wolf, 'it goes against the grain
That for a cheese this fellow's off the hook.'
'Sir,' said the fox, 'you ought not to complain
For, by my soul, you are the one at fault.'
'Then,' said the wolf, 'I'm finished with the plot;
But I'd like to see this cheese you boast about.'
'Sir,' said the fox, 'he told me where it's kept.'

Then hand in hand they go on to a hill.
The farmer to his farmhouse takes his way,
Glad to have eluded their ill will,
And stands guard by his door till break of day.
So let us turn to the others now as they
Proceed through lonely woods, two footsore prowlers
From bush to bush well into the small hours.

All through the long night Lawrence wracks his wits
How he might pacify the wolf by guile.
His promise of the cheese he now regrets
But in the end he hits upon a wile
So satisfactory he has to smile.
'This is blind man's buff,' wolf says, 'my friend.
We hunt all night, but not a thing we find.'

'Sir,' said the fox, 'we are all but there.
Stop worrying and you shall see it soon.'
They hurried on until they reached a manor.
Like a new penny shone the full round moon.
Then to a draw-well these two gents are come
Where a bucket hung at each end of the rope.
As the one went down the other was cranked up.

The schadow off the mone schone in the well:
'Schir,' said Lowrence, 'anis ye sall find me leill;
Now se ye not the caboik weill yoursell,
Quhyte as ane neip and round als as ane seill?
He hang it yonder that na man suld it steill.
Schir, traist ye weill, yone caboik ye se hing
Micht be ane present to ony lord or king.'

'Na,' quod the wolff, 'mycht I yone caboik haif
On the dry land, as I it yonder se,
I wald quitclame the carll off all the laif:
His dart oxin I compt thame not ane fle;
Yone wer mair meit for sic ane man as me.
Lowrence,' quod he, 'leip in the bukket sone,
And I sall hald the ane, quhill thow have done.'

Lowrence gird doun baith sone and subtellie;
The uther baid abufe and held the flaill.
'It is sa mekill', quod Lowrence, 'it maisteris me:
On all my tais it hes not left ane naill.
Ye man mak help upwart, and it haill:
Leip in the uther bukket haistelie,
And cum sone doun and mak me sum supplé!'

Than lychtlie in the bukket lap the loun;
His wecht but weir the uther end gart ryis:
The tod come hailland up, the wolff yeid doun.
Than angerlie the wolff upon him cryis:
'I cummand thus dounwart, quhy thow upwart hyis?'
'Schir,' quod the foxe, 'thus fairis it off Fortoun:
As ane cummis up, scho quheillis ane uther doun.'

The moon's reflection shone deep in the well.
'Sir,' said the fox, 'for once you'll find me true.
Now don't you see the cheese there, visible,
White as a turnip, round as a seal, although
He hung it deep to keep it hid from view?
For this cheese, sir, believe me, is a thing
Would make a gift for any lord or king.'

'Ah,' said the wolf, 'if I could have yon cheese
Out high and dry in its entirety
I'd let yon clown off everything he owes.
What good's a dumb ox team? I set him free.
Yon cheese is more the fare for men like me.
Lawrence,' he cried, 'into that bucket, quick,
And I will hold on here, then wind you back.'

Quickly, dexterously the fox leaps in.
The other stays to keep hold of the handle.
'It's so immense,' says fox, 'it has me beaten.
My toes won't grip, I've torn off every nail.
You'll have to help me up. Such a huge haul!
Get into that other bucket and descend
This minute to me here and lend a hand.'

Nimbly then the idiot leapt in
Which made, of course, the other bucket rise.
The fox was hoisted up, the wolf wound down.
And as they pass wolf furiously cries,
'Why is my bucket falling while yours flies?'
'Sir,' said the fox, 'it's thus with Fortune ever,
If she lets one soar, she's like to sink another.'

Than to the ground sone yeid the wolff in haist;
The tod lap on land, als blyith as ony bell,
And left the wolff in watter to the waist:
Quha haillit him out, I wait not, off the well.
Heir endis the text; thair is na mair to tell.
Yyt men may find ane gude moralitie
In this sentence, thocht it ane fabill be.

MORALITAS

This wolf I likkin to ane wickit man
Quhilk dois the pure oppres in everie place,
And pykis at thame all querrellis that he can,
Be rigour, reif, and uther wickitnes.
The foxe, the feind I call into this cais,
Arctand ilk man to ryn unrychteous rinkis,
Thinkand thairthrow to lok him in his linkis.

The husband may be callit ane godlie man
With quhome the feynd falt findes, as clerkis reids,
Besie to tempt him with all wayis that he can.
The hennis ar warkis that fra ferme faith proceidis:
Quhair sic sproutis spreidis, the evill spreit thair not speidis,
Bot wendis unto the wickit man agane –
That he hes tint his travell is full unfane.

The wodds waist, quhairin wes the wolf wyld,
Ar wickit riches, quhilk all men gaipis to get:
Quha traistis in sic trusterie ar oft begyld,
For mammon may be callit the devillis net,
Quhilk Sathanas for all sinfull hes set:
With proud plesour quha settis his traist thairin,
But speciall grace lychtlie can not outwin.

Down to the bottom then the wolf shot past
While Lawrence lands on top, a happy fox
Leaving the wolf in water to the waist.
To tell who rescued him, I'm at a loss.
The text ends here. There is no further gloss.
Except that men may find morality
In this narration, fable though it be.

MORALITAS

This wolf I liken to a wicked man,
Oppressor of the poor, a callous bully,
Involving them in every quarrel he can,
Extortionate, harsh, and full of cruelty.
And fox is devil in the allegory,
Inveigling into viciousness the man
He would lead to ruin on his lock and chain.

The farmer may be classed a godly man
With whom the fiend finds fault (as scholars warn),
Waylaying him at all times with temptation.
The hens are works from firm faith bred and born.
Where such things sprout, evil is spurned and turned
Back on the evildoer once again,
Who ends up an embittered, angry man.

The lonely woods where the wolf was hoodwinked
Are corrupting riches all men long to get
But fail to see they're trash, not worth a trinket,
For riches may be called the Devil's Net
Which Satan has for sinners stretched and set.
Without a special grace, indulgent man
Can never be absolved of sins of Mammon.

The cabok may be callit covetyce,
Quhilk blomis braid in mony mannis ee:
Wa worth the well of that wickit vyce,
For it is all bot fraud and fantasie,
Dryvand ilk man to leip in the buttrie
That dounwart drawis unto the pane of hell –
Christ keip all Christianis from that wickit well!

The cheese may be denoted covetousness,
Ever in full bloom in many an eye.
Cursed be the well that incubates that vice
For all it is is fraud and fantasy,
Driving men wild into the buttery
That drags and draws them down to burning hell –
Christ keep all Christians from that wicked well.

UPON ANE TYME, as Esope culd report,
Ane lytill mous come till ane rever-syde:
Scho micht not waid, hir schankis wer sa schort;
Scho culd not swym; scho had na hors to ryde;
Off verray force behovit hir to byde;
And to and fra besyde that revir deip
Scho ran, cryand with mony pietuous peip.

'Help over! Help over!' this silie mous can cry,
'For Goddis lufe, sum bodie, over the brym.'
With that ane paddok, in the watter by,
Put up hir heid and on the bank can clym,
Quhilk be nature culd douk and gaylie swym.
With voce full rauk, scho said on this maneir:
'Gude morne, schir Mous! Quhat is your erand heir?'

'Seis thow', quod scho, 'off corne yone jolie flat,
Off ryip aitis, off barlie, peis, and quheit?
I am hungrie, and fane wald be thairat,
Bot I am stoppit be this watter greit;
And on this syde I get nathing till eit
Bot hard nuttis, quhilkis with my teith I bore:
Wer I beyond, my feist wer fer the more.

The Toad and the Mouse

UPON A TIME, as Aesop makes report,
A little mouse came to a riverside.
She couldn't wade, her mouse-shanks were so short,
She couldn't swim, she had no horse to ride,
So willy-nilly there she had to bide
And to and fro beside that river deep
She ran and cried with many a piteous *peep*.

'Help, help me over,' cried the poor wee mouse,
'For love of God, someone, across this stream.'
With that a toad, in water nearby, rose
(For toads by nature nimbly duck and swim),
And showed her head to mount the bank and come
Croaking ashore, then gave her greetings thus:
'Good morning! And what brings you here, Miss Mouse?'

'The corn', she said, 'in yon field, do you see it?
The ripened oats, the barley, peas and wheat?
I'm hungry and I'd love to get to it
But the water here's too wide, so here I sit
And on this side get not a thing to eat
But hard nuts that I have to gnaw and bore.
Over beyond, I'd feast on better fare.

'I have no boit; heir is no maryner;
And thocht thair war, I have no fraucht to pay.'
Quod scho, 'Sister, lat be your hevie cheir;
Do my counsall, and I sall find the way,
Withoutin hors, brig, boit, or yit galay,
To bring yow over saiflie, be not afeird –
And not wetand the campis off your beird.'

'I haif grit wounder', quod the lytill mous,
'How can thow fleit without fedder or fin?
This rever is sa deip and dangerous,
Me think that thow suld droun to wed thairin.
Tell me, thairfoir, quhat facultie or gin
Thow hes to bring the over this watter wan.'
That to declair the paddok thus began:

'With my twa feit,' quod scho, 'lukkin and braid,
Insteid off airis, I row the streme full styll,
And thocht the brym be perrillous to waid,
Baith to and fra I swyme at my awin will,
I may not droun, forquhy my oppin gill
Devoidis ay the watter I resaiff:
Thairfoir to droun, forsuith, na dreid I haif.'

The mous beheld unto hir fronsit face,
Hir runkillit cheikis, and hir lippis syde,
Hir hingand browis, and hir voce sa hace,
Hir loggerand leggis, and hir harsky hyde.
Scho ran abak, and on the paddok cryde:
'Giff I can ony skill off phisnomy,
Thow hes sumpart off falset and invy.

'I have no boat, there is no ferryman,
And if there were, I have no coin to pay.'
'Sister,' said toad, 'would you stop worrying.
Do what I tell you and I shall find a way
Without horse, bridge or boat or any ferry
To get you over safely, never fear –
And not wet once a whisker or a hair.'

'I greatly wonder', said the little mouse,
'How you can, without fin or feather, float.
This river is so deep and dangerous
I think you'd drown as soon as you'd wade out.
Tell me, therefore, what is the gift or secret
You own to bring you over this dark flood?'
And thus in explanation spoke the toad:

'With my two feet for oars, webbed and broad,
I row the stream,' she said, 'and quietly pull,
And though it's deep and dangerous to wade,
I swim it to and fro at my own will
And cannot sink, because my open gill
Vents and voids the water I breathe in.
So truly, I am not afraid to drown.'

The mouse gazed up into her furrowed face,
Her wrinkled cheeks, her ridged lips like a lid
Hasped shut on her hoarse voice, her hanging brows,
Her lanky wobbly legs and wattled hide;
Then, taken aback, she faced the toad and cried,
'If I know any physiognomy,
The signs on you are of untruth and envy.

'*For clerkis sayis the inclinatioun*
Off mannis thocht proceidis commounly
Efter the corporall complexioun
To gude or evill, as nature will apply:
Ane thrawart will, ane thrawin phisnomy.
The auld proverb is witnes off this lorum:
Distortum vultum sequitur distortio morum.'

'*Na,*' *quod the taid,* '*that proverb is not trew,*
For fair thingis oftymis ar fundin faikin;
The blaberyis, thocht thay be sad off hew,
Ar gadderit up quhen primeros is forsakin;
The face may faill to be the hartis takin;
Thairfoir I find this scripture in all place:
"*Thow suld not juge ane man efter his face.*"

'*Thocht I unhailsum be to luke upon,*
I have na wyt; quhy suld I lakkit be?
Wer I als fair as jolie Absolon,
I am no causer off that grit beutie;
This difference in forme and qualitie
Almychtie God hes causit dame Nature
To prent and set in everilk creature.

'*Off sum the face may be full flurischand,*
Off silkin toung and cheir rycht amorous,
With mynd inconstant, fals, and wariand,
Full off desait and menis cautelous.'
'*Let be thy preiching,*' *quod the hungrie mous,*
'*And be quhat craft, thow gar me understand,*
That thow wald gyde me to yone yonder land.'

'For scholars say the main inclination
Of a man's thought will usually proceed
According to the corporal complexion,
The good or evil prompting in the blood.
A thrawn feature means a nature twisted.
The Latin tag affords a proof of this –
Mores, it says, are mirrored in the face.'

'No,' said the toad, 'that proverb isn't true,
For what looks good is often a false showing.
The bilberry may have a dreary hue
But will be picked while primrose is left growing.
The face may fail to be the heart's true token.
Therefore I find this judgement still applies:
"You shouldn't judge a man just by his face."

'Unwholesome as I am to look upon,
It's not my fault. Why should people blame me?
Were I as fair as lovely Absalom,
I won't have been the cause of my own beauty.
This difference in form and quality
God Almighty has caused Mother Nature
To print and inset into every creature.

'Some people's faces may shine eagerly,
Their tongues be silken, their manner sweet and douce,
Yet they are insubstantial inwardly,
Deceitful, unreliable and false.'
'Let be your preaching,' cried the hungry mouse.
'Just make it clear to me how you intend
To guide me over to that bank beyond.'

'Thow wait,' quod scho, 'ane bodie that hes neid
To help thameself suld mony wayis cast.
Thairfoir ga tak ane doubill twynit threid
And bind thy leg to myne with knottis fast:
I sall the leir to swym – be not agast –
Als weill as I.' 'As thow?' than quod the mous.
'To preif that play, it wer rycht perrillous!

'Suld I be bund and fast, quhar I am fre,
In hoip off help? Na, than I schrew us baith,
For I mycht lois baith lyfe and libertie!
Giff it wer swa, quha suld amend the skaith.
Bot gif thow sweir to me the murthour-aith:
But fraud or gyle to bring me over this flude,
But hurt or harme?' 'In faith,' quod scho, 'I dude.'

Scho goikit up, and to the hevin can cry:
'How! Juppiter, off nature god and king,
I mak ane aith trewlie to the, that I
This lytill mous sall over this watter bring.'
This aith wes maid; the mous, but persaving
The fals ingyne of this foull-carpand pad,
Tuke threid and band hir leg, as scho hir bad.

Than fute for fute thay lap baith in the brym,
Bot in thair myndis thay wer rycht different:
The mous thocht nathing bot to fleit and swym;
The paddok for to droun set hir intent.
Quhen thay in midwart off the streme wer went,
With all hir force the paddok preissit doun,
And thocht the mous without mercie to droun.

'You know,' the toad said, 'whenever people need
To help themselves, they should think resourcefully.
Go therefore, take a double twine of thread
And bind your leg to mine and knot it firmly.
I'll teach you how to swim – no, no, don't worry –
As well as I.' 'As you?' replied the mouse.
'To play that game could prove most dangerous.

'I have my freedom, hope for help, but why
Should I be bound? Bad cess then to us both!
For I might lose both life and liberty
And then who's going to compensate that loss –
Unless you swear to me by life and death
To bring me safe and sound to the other side
Without cheating.' 'I'll do it,' said the toad

And rolled her eyes to heaven and gave a cry,
'O Jupiter, god and king of nature,
This oath I swear in truth to you, that I
Will bring this little mouse across the water.'
The oath was made. The mouse, who knew no better
Than to trust the fork-tongued falsehoods of this toad,
Took thread and bound her leg as she was bid.

Then both in step, they leapt into the stream,
But in their minds it was a different case.
The mouse's one thought was to float and swim.
To drown the mouse the toad had set her face
And when they reached midstream, started to press
Downward on her, with every ounce of force,
And mercilessly tried to sink the mouse.

Persavand this, the mous on hir can cry:
'Tratour to God, and manesworne unto me!
Thow swore the murthour-aith richt now that I
But hurt or harme suld ferryit be and fre.'
And quhen scho saw thair wes bot do or de,
Scho bowtit up and forsit hir to swym,
And preissit upon the taiddis bak to clym.

The dreid of deith hir strenthis gart incres,
And forcit hir defend with mycht and mane.
The mous upwart, the paddok doun can pres;
Quhyle to, quhyle fra, quhyle doukit up agane.
This selie mous, this plungit in grit pane,
Gan fecht als lang as breith wes in hir breist,
Till at the last scho cryit for ane preist.

Fechtand thusgait, the gled sat on ane twist,
And to this wretchit battell tuke gude heid;
And with ane wisk or owthir off thame wist
He claucht his cluke betuix thame in the threid;
Syne to the land he flew with thame gude speid,
Fane off that fang, pyipand with mony pew,
Syne lowsit thame, and baith but pietie slew.

Syne bowellit thame, that boucheour with his bill,
And bellieflaucht full fettislie thame fled,
Bot all thair flesche wald scant be half ane fill,
And guttis als, unto that gredie gled.
Off thair debait thus quhen I hard outred,
He tuke his flicht and over the feildis flaw.
Giff this be trew, speir ye at thame that saw.

Perceiving this, the mouse cried in dismay,
'Traitor to God! False witness! Perjurer!
Just now you swore by life and death that I
Would be ferried safe and sound across the water.'
But when she realised this was a matter
Of do or die, she scrambled hard to swim
And on the toad's back fought to cling and climb.

The fear of death had made her that much stronger.
In self-defence she fought with might and main.
The mouse strained up, the toad pressed down upon her,
Now to, now fro, now sunk, now safe again.
And so this poor mouse, plunged in such great pain,
Struggled as long as breath was in her breast
Till in the end she called out for a priest.

As they were battling on like this, a kite
Roosting upon a branch nearby took heed
And before they knew what happened made a strike
And clenched his claw between them round the thread,
Then swept them to the bank with all good speed,
Pleased with his prey, repeating his kite-call,
Then loosed them both and made a cruel kill.

That butcher disembowelled them with his bill,
Flayed them, stripped the skin off inside out
Like taking off a sock, but, guts and all,
They could no more than whet his appetite.
Then, having thus decided their debate,
He rose from the field, I hear, and off he flew.
Ask whoever saw if this be true.

MORALITAS

My brother, gif thow will tak advertence,
Be this fabill thow may persave and se
It passis far all kynd of pestilence
Ane wickit mynd with wordis fair and sle.
Be war thairfore with quhome thow fallowis the,
For thow wer better beir of stane the barrow,
Or sueitand dig and delf quhill thow may dre,
Than to be matchit with ane wickit marrow.

Ane fals intent under ane fair pretence
Hes causit mony innocent for to de;
Grit folie is to gif over-sone credence
To all that speiks fairlie unto the;
Ane silkin toung, ane hart of crueltie,
Smytis more sore than ony schot of arrow;
Brother, gif thow be wyse, I reid the fle
To matche the with ane thrawart fenyeit marrow.

I warne the als, it is grit nekligence
To bind the fast quhair thow wes frank and fre:
Fra thow be bund, thow may mak na defence
To saif thy lyfe nor yit thy libertie.
This simpill counsall, brother, tak at me,
And it to cun perqueir se thow not tarrow:
Better but stryfe to leif allane in le
Than to be matchit with ane wickit marrow.

This hald in mynd – rycht more I sall the tell
Quhairby thir beistis may be figurate.
The paddok, usand in the flude to duell,
Is mannis bodie, swymand air and late

MORALITAS

Now, my brother, if you pay attention
And study this last fable, you will see
How honeyed words that hide a false intention
Surpass all else in pure malignity,
So when you choose your friends, beware, be canny
For you'd better wheel a barrow full of stones
And bear the brunt and sweat it out all day
Than associate with bad companions.

A kindly face can mask maliciousness
And often brings the innocent to grief.
It's better to think twice, act cautious,
Suspect all blandishment, suspend belief.
Silken tongues are snares for the naif:
Fledged and barbed like arrows, they can wound.
So, brother, best beware and have no truck with
A crooked, double-dealing, two-faced friend.

I warn you also, it is a great mistake
To bind yourself when you're at large and free,
Since once you're bound, your very life's at stake,
You will have forfeited your liberty.
Brother, this simple warning take from me,
Remember it and learn it like your lessons:
Better be banished to live on lonely lea
Than associate with bad companions.

Attend to this: and I have more to tell
About the meanings these beasts represent.
The toad, at home in water, is natural
Man in this world, in his mortal element,

Into this warld, with cairis implicate:
Now hie, now law, quhylis plungit up, quhylis doun,
Ay in perrell, and reddie for to droun;

Now dolorus, now blyth as bird on breir;
Now in fredome, now wardit in distres;
Now haill and sound, now deid and brocht on beir;
Now pure as Job, now rowand in riches;
Now gounis gay, now brats laid in pres;
Now full as fische, now hungrie as ane hound;
Now on the quheill, now wappit to the ground.

This lytill mous, heir knit thus be the schyn,
The saull of man betakin may indeid –
Bundin, and fra the bodie may not twyn,
Quhill cruell deith cum brek of lyfe the threid –
The quhilk to droun suld ever stand in dreid
Of carnall lust be the suggestioun,
Quhilk drawis ay the saull and druggis doun.

The watter is the warld, ay welterand
With mony wall of tribulatioun,
In quhilk the saull and bodye wer steirrand,
Standand distinyt in thair opinioun:
The spreit upwart, the body precis doun;
The saull rycht fane wald be brocht over, iwis,
Out of this warld into the hevinnis blis.

The gled is deith, that cummis suddandlie
As dois ane theif, and cuttis sone the battall:
Be vigilant thairfoir and ay reddie,
For mannis lyfe is brukill and ay mortall.
My freind, thairfoir, mak the ane strang castell

Aswim in sorrow, doomed to discontent:
Now high, now low, whiles lifted up, whiles down,
Always in peril, liable to drown.

Now sorrowful, now singing like a bird
Free betimes, betimes a captive spirit;
Now sound of health, now laid out in the morgue;
Now poor as Job, now lavish and elated;
Now in old rags, now rakishly outfitted,
Now a fed fish and now a famished hound;
Now Fortune's wheel and now the hard low ground.

This little mouse, tied up here by the shin
May signify the soul of man indeed,
Trapped in flesh and locked in body's prison.
Till death arrives to cut the living thread
Soul must be vigilant, must stand in dread
Of carnal lust that lures and tempts it down
And presses, pulls, loads, drags until it drown.

The water is the world, a turbulence
Of surging woe and waves of tribulation
Through which the soul and body must advance,
Distinct and different in their inclination:
Soul pushes up, the body presses down.
Soul's whole desire is to be borne across
Out of this world to heaven, into bliss.

The kite is death, that comes suddenly
Out of the blue to conclude the battle.
Therefore be on guard and always ready
For human life is shaky, fragile, mortal.
And you, my friend, fortify soul's castle

Of gud deidis, for deith will the assay,
Thow wait not quhen – evin, morrow, or midday.

Adew, my friend, and gif that ony speiris
Of this fabill, sa schortlie I conclude,
Say thow, I left the laif unto the freiris,
To mak a sample or similitude.
Now Christ for us that deit on the rude,
Of saull and lyfe as thow art Salviour,
Grant us till pas intill ane blissit hour.

With good deeds, since there's no telling when
Death will attack you: morning, evening, noon.

Adieu then, friend, and if anyone enquires
About this fable I hasten to conclude,
Say it's to be continued by the friars
As an example or similitude.
And now, dear Christ, who died upon the rood,
Saviour of life and soul, grant that we pass
Happily through death in a state of grace.